T0367724

DIVIDE
AND
CONQUER

Target Your Customers
through Market Segmentation

Harry Webber

John Wiley & Sons, Inc.

New York • Chichester • Weinheim • Brisbane • Singapore • Toronto

Published by John Wiley & Sons, Inc.
Published simultaneously in Canada.

No part of this publication may be reproduced, stored in a retrieval system or transmitted in any form or by any means, electronic, mechanical, photocopying, recording, scanning or otherwise, except as permitted under Sections 107 or 108 of the 1976 United States Copyright Act, without either the prior written permission of the Publisher, or authorization through payment of the appropriate per-copy fee to the Copyright Clearance Center, 222 Rosewood Drive, Danvers, MA 01923, (978) 750-8400, fax (978) 750-4744. Requests to the Publisher for permission should be addressed to the Permissions Department, John Wiley & Sons, Inc., 605 Third Avenue, New York, NY 10158-0012, (212) 850-6011, fax (212) 850-6008, E-Mail: PERMREQ@WILEY.COM.

This publication is designed to provide accurate and authoritative information in regard to the subject matter covered. It is sold with the understanding that the publisher is not engaged in rendering legal, accounting, or other professional services. If legal advice or other expert assistance is required, the services of a competent professional person should be sought.

Library of Congress Cataloging-in-Publication Data:
Webber, Harry, 1944–
    Divide and conquer : target your customers through market
segmentation / Harry Webber.
      p.   cm.
    Includes index.
    ISBN 0-471-17633-8 (cloth : alk. paper)
    1. Market segmentation—United States. I. Title.
HF5415.127.W4   1998
658.8′02—dc21
                                      98-19880
                                          CIP

Acknowledgments

I would like to thank several people for helping in the preparation of this book. First I must acknowledge my mom, Bernice Webber, who first inspired me to seek a career on Madison Avenue, and my business partner, Monica L. Erne, who suggested I write these Madison Avenue war stories and was my first editor. Ruth Mills at John Wiley & Sons, whose patience, editorial guidance, and inspiration were invaluable for a writer who has never written anything longer than than a 60-second TV spot. Development editor Janice G. Borzendowski, who helped me mold these case studies into a readable manuscript, deserves a special debt of gratitude. Also, a hearty thanks is due my mentors Berry Gordy, Jr., Helmut Krone, Gene Case, Mike Becker, Alex Kroll, Jim Lawrence, Bob Wilvers, Tom Burrell, Fernando Tomayo, and Bob Levin, without whom I never could have gained the experiences that were worth writing about in the first place.

Contents

Introduction

Imagine having a terrific product to sell and a captive audience of 100 possible prospects to sell it to. Which way would you move more product? Would you have one salesperson stand on a chair with a microphone and pitch the entire room at the same time? Or would you instruct 20 salespeople to work their way through the crowd, meeting and greeting folks, acquainting themselves with the most likely customers, then figuring out exactly what it would take to get them to say yes to the product?

If you chose the latter scenario, then you understand the basic concept behind segmented, or selective, marketing, a powerful and necessary weapon for any marketer to master in the 2000s. If, however, you chose scenario number one, you still believe in the principles of mass marketing, and I offer this book as an important—make that *essential*—alternative to that tradition. A wake-up call. To maintain the pace of change in today's splintering marketplace, product and service campaigns can no longer survive on "one-pitch-fits-all" marketing strategies. Markets must be efficiently selected before they can be effectively sold.

Now is the time for your company to grow bigger by thinking smaller. Today, many well-informed problem-solving companies are sharing meaningful information with groups of like-minded consumers through the efficiencies of selective marketing. Slowly but surely, these companies are gaining ground on their mass-marketing competitors, who are still spending millions trying to make a single pitch hit vast numbers of very different individuals.

Practitioners of selective marketing build *relationships,* which will continue to grow while mass-market competitors' sales begin to plateau. Those relationships will open the door to other relationships, and as you address their ever changing needs, you will grow your business. As the number of selected market segments addressed by your selective marketing program increases, so too will your knowledge of your product's or service's place in their lives.

This book is an anecdotal overview of some famous (and not so famous) brand building campaigns from the viewpoint of the person responsible for creating consumer relationships for those brands. This is not a numbers book because I consider my clients' numbers to be proprietary, as do they. Suffice it to say that the brands covered in this book are leaders in their respective product categories. This book is about the insights gained in the process of generating those leadership positions by those who were on the front lines.

This is about how to go from here to there, market segment by market segment. This book will take you from the boardrooms of Madison Avenue and Detroit to the killing fields of the South Bronx and Watts. It addresses the mind-set of those who live for the latest NBA scores to the hope of those who are living with AIDS. We look inside of the heads of people of wealth and people who play with trains. SMART always looks for common threads to tie each client's brand to. This is the work of selective marketing.

Because memory is imperfect, I apologize in advance for any factual errors or omissions. Feel free to E-mail any corrections or comments (or business) you may have to smartcommco@earthlink .net, and we will post those corrections and comments (the good ones) at www.smartcomm.com/dncupdate. Aside from that important disclaimer from our lawyers, I hope you enjoy the ride.

Divide and Conquer was written for senior corporate marketing managers. You are the selected market for this book. In it, I share the tactics utilized by selective market experts to effectively and efficiently define, infiltrate, and motivate the principal societal, cultural, and demographic segments of our domestic marketplace. Selective marketing can lead to the captivating, meaningful, inventive communications efforts that capture an audience's imagination wherever they are encountered.

> **SMART Marketing:**
> ___
>
> **Practitioners of selective marketing seek to build relationships with individual market segments; mass marketers aim broadly and hope to hit as many customers as possible with a single pitch.**

SMART (an acronym for Selective Marketing Advertising Research Technologies) is one of the first marketing communications firms to specialize in segmented, or selective, marketing. Since 1986, I and my colleagues have dedicated ourselves to the development and refinement of selective marketing: *the practice of motivating action through intensive intelligence gathering.* Determining who are the most likely prospects for our clients' products or services and influencing their perception of our clients' abilities to meet their needs and fulfill their desires are the essence of selective marketing. Our research, creative, and media teams have been called the "thought police" by some of our clients, in reference to the attention we pay to the details that define each consumer individually—*selectively.*

> **SMART Marketing:**
> ___
>
> **Selective marketing motivates action through intensive intelligence gathering to determine our selected consumer's personal (or professional) wants, needs, and desires.**

Once we have accurately identified the target customer's needs, values, and preferences, our thought police quantify the purchase patterns of our client's selected market. They evaluate the efficiency of the selected market's principal media, then put that information to work to develop a mutually beneficial and supportive long-term product or service relationship program. The definition of the target market may comprise any number of the traditional segmentation categories dominated by the prevailing interest categories with which the targeted consumer most closely identifies.

THE SIGNIFICANCE OF THE INDIVIDUAL

This is a book about values. *Divide and Conquer* examines the business practice of identifying the American public's innermost values and beliefs, one at a time, and then using that knowledge to initiate, navigate, influence, and maintain consumer relationships with those most likely to say yes to your client's product or service. You will come to understand how and why consumer insights and information regarding personal opinion and attitude are being utilized by astute selective marketers. You will learn how to utilize such information in determining which methodologies are most effective in motivating your selected market segment to act.

To experts of niche marketing and a growing number of Fortune 500/1000 sales executives, mass marketing is becoming an outmoded concept in American business. They are learning from experience that marketing must become increasingly pluralistic and decidedly less monolithic if they are to build strong and loyal customer bases. To ensure the viability of their brands in the long term, many former mass marketers are utilizing selective marketing programs for the obvious—but often overlooked—fact: Different folks need different strokes.

America's fragmenting marketplace is being tracked, studied, and sold with the precision of a smart bomb. Segment by segment, group by group, and individual by individual, markets are being identified, defined, focus-grouped, mall-intercepted, phone-polled, quantified, qualified, analyzed, redefined, and targeted with the appropriate strategy, creative, media, and evaluation apparatuses. Hitting these targets efficiently and repeatedly is one of the most challenging tasks facing America's marketing communications and media decision makers in the next millennium.

Conquering the new marketing frontier in the coming century will require an astute understanding of and facility with the "relevant realities" of many diversified consumer networks. In other words, the realities facing an African-American, low-income, rural teen are considerably different from the realities facing a WASP, wealthy, gay man in his mid-40s. Both realities are relevant to both prospective consumers. But generally, the realities facing one of these consumers are of no interest or consequence to the other. That's why we have to dig, dig, dig. Dig? Consider the state of the marketing profession in the late 1990s. A Yankelovich, Clancy, Shulman (the internationally renowned and respected marketing research firm) study of marketers, market researchers, and chief executives of Fortune 1000 firms for the American Marketing Association revealed that the majority of those polled no longer believed that

- To be successful a product must have mass appeal.
- Marketing is a textbook science as opposed to an art.
- Advertising is the most effective marketing tool.
- The best product wins the biggest market share.
- Good marketing can sell any product.

In short, this study revealed what proponents of selective marketing already knew: Mass marketing and the traditional marketing resources are no longer capable of coming up with the solutions that solve the problems of how to move product successfully in the current era. In a rush to "reengineer" themselves into leaner, meaner, and decidedly younger mirrors of their clients, traditional marketing firms have simply used up their intellectual capital, which we at SMART define as the ability to generate ideas capable of inspiring sales and fueling growth. Furthermore, they have done this without making the investment in technologies that might help them replenish this critical asset. That is to say that many of the nation's top-rated advertising agencies have succumbed to the "brain drain" brought on by tighter marketing budgets, falling fees and commissions, and the scrutiny of public ownership. Money got tight and Madison Avenue rejected expensive, experienced practitioners for considerably cheaper "fresh blood." The intellectual capital that went into building the megabrands was out. New was in. As a result, mass marketers are now floundering to answer critical questions posed by our rapidly changing society; for example, what does the increase in smoking among young people mean to the health care industry? How does the rise in sexually transmitted diseases affect the birth rate? Important questions like these are generating "best guess" answers from the nation's mass marketing practitioners. To date, the results of this brain drain have been an 80 percent failure rate in domestic new product introductions, according to Bill Gorman's *New Product News*.

> **SMART Marketing:**
>
> Hitting these targets efficiently, meaningfully, and repeatedly is one of the most challenging tasks facing America's marketing communications and media decision makers in the next millennium.

In their book, *The Marketing Revolution* (HarperBusiness, 1991), Kevin J. Clancy and Robert Shulman, former chairman and CEO, respectively, of Yankelovich, challenged the way media are traditionally priced and evaluated. In the case of television advertising, for example, they suggest that astute buyers base their decisions on cost per thousand people *involved* in a television program, as opposed to cost per thousand people *exposed* to a television program. In their CPM/CPMI comparison of the ten top-rated programs, buying "involved" viewers resulted in a significant 18.5 percent cost savings.

Perhaps even more significant was a study of 470 randomly selected female heads of households subjected to programs and commercials in conditions that mimicked normal in-home viewing conditions. Clancy and Shulman were able to construct a reliable program involvement measure. The object of their study was to establish an entertainment value for different programs. Concurrent with this measure, they also calculated for the commercial's unaided recall, aided copy point recall, credibility for each message recalled, and purchase interest. This study concluded that as program involvement goes up, all five commercial or advertising measures also go up. This is a chilling indicator for those mass marketers who have long preached the mantra, "more is better." This study proves that, today, more just costs more. Involved is better.

This book attempts to explain, through case studies, how selective marketing establishes ongoing consumer relationships through *collective experiences*—the sum takeaway after the selected consumer has been exposed to a specific series of meaningful impressions—that help products and services meet and exceed the needs and expectations of their most likely customers.

DEFINE YOUR SELECTED MARKET

Before you can approach a selected market, you must familiarize yourself with the physical, emotional, cultural, and intellectual environment in which that market exists. It is of critical importance that you gain a clear understanding of the forces at work in the market before determining where your product or service can be most successfully positioned to meet the needs of your targeted consumers. You need to understand

- Why the lack of knowledge about your product translates to a no-sell—in any language
- That advertising must talk to its market, not its makers
- That an insider's understanding of your targeted market segment gives you the ability to convey your product or service as both different and better than your competitor's
- How emotions impact a consumer's decision to purchase
- That identifying your targeted segment's emotional needs and wants is an ongoing effort, because those needs and wants change—sometimes frequently; and sometimes you may even have to rework an in-progress campaign or start over to ensure that it reflects the changing face of your target market

You Just Don't Understand Me

"You just don't understand me." It's the sentence that has spelled the end of countless personal relationships. And for a marketer who doesn't truly understand his or her client's target customer, the result is the same: the end of the relationship. I repeat: Selective marketing is the process of building relationships between your brand and your brand's target consumers, and you can't do that unless you understand what makes them tick.

The concept is hardly new. For centuries, astute merchants and wandering peddlers have sent "shills" ahead into target towns to find out which merchandise they should have on display when entering the town square. A more organized and well-known example of this practice came on the heels of World War II, when, according to the *Los Angeles Times,* a Japanese firm sent undercover "spies" to learn the automotive habits and needs of American suburbanites. By finding out what the customers wanted—while Detroit's Big Three were busy competing among themselves—the Japanese ultimately changed the face of the international automotive market and brought an end to American dominance in the automotive industry.

Understanding Your Target Customer Is Your First Job

But how do you get there from here? The extent to which it is necessary to go to track down the most likely prospects for our clients' selected markets is not for the faint of heart. At SMART, for example, we have gone one on one in gang territory; we've eavesdropped in ladies' rooms; if the client wants to build a relationship with locomotive engineers, somebody from SMART is climbing into the locomotive. Selective marketing is not passive, ivory-tower number crunching. Selective marketing is knowing their names, speaking their language, and understanding their needs, then fulfilling them faster, better, cheaper than the competitors.

Simply put, *everything* about selective marketing is based on

- Identifying the differences that define the characteristics of a market segment

- Knowing what is needed to transform a population segment into a viable market segment

- Learning that *qualitative,* rather than quantitative, research enlightens

- Recognizing and addressing the fact that, for certain products and services, customers may make an emotional decision, then justify it intellectually

- Acknowledging the power that peer or social approval has on some customers' decision to buy

- Realizing that managing a market segment means you must work at the local, not the global, level

> **SMART Marketing:**
>
> Selective marketing means knowing their names, speaking their language, and understanding their needs, then fulfilling them faster, better, cheaper than your competitors.

MOTIVATION

Motivation is a fascinating subject. What makes people do the things they do? Like a detective seeking the motive behind a crime before he or she can determine likely suspects, selective marketers, too, must detect what is and is not relevant to their selected prospects before beginning the task of understanding what motivates their actions. They must learn

- Why prospects won't buy from a name they don't trust

- How bonds of trust are built within a targeted market segment

- The importance of social sensitivity in the development of a segmented marketing strategy

- Why immersing yourself in the "cultural ecosystem" of the market segment is essential before you initiate a marketing program

- Why you need to determine the effectiveness of the segment's marketing channels before you set up distribution

- The effect of cultural, professional, or geographic behavior patterns on awareness and retention of your sales message

- Exactly what makes a product, service, person, idea, or issue meaningful and relevant to the target audience, and where to start building that relevance

- How to motivate a new segment of the market without alienating your current customers

What must selective marketers do to peel away the layers of resistance and motivate the decision to act—in this case, to buy or partake of a service? How can we influence that decision in our favor? Some of the answers are here.

ONE SIZE FITS ONE

One-to-one marketing. Personalized content. These are popular buzz phrases used to describe media that give you only the information that interests you, whether it's financial briefs custom-tailored to your investment strategy, sports scores of only those teams you cheer for, background on film noir movie classics of the 1940s and 1950s. But there's another buzz phrase getting its share of ink recently: *global marketing*. World brands have built elaborate infrastructures around this concept, believing that global marketing will make their mass-marketing efforts even more massive. They cite satellite television and the Internet as proof that their goals are not only possible, but practical as well. We at SMART beg to differ. One size does *not* fit all. Just ask any woman who has ever tried to wear one-size-fits-all pantyhose.

Once we were a product of our environment. Now we are becoming environments for our products. Mass marketing is becoming irrelevant in such a fragmented society. It is even difficult today to get anyone to actually admit to being a member of the "masses." Oh, they'll tell you they're working class or middle class or Chicago Bulls fans. Some will even own up to being members of the silent majority or the baby-boom generation, or viewers of *The X-Files*. But ask them if they consider themselves part of the masses. Nobody wants to be "mass" anything. They all feel that they and their peer group are somehow special, different.

Perhaps even more important than feelings of "specialness" is that advances in computer technologies have given the public at large access to many of the same tools of media creation and the wide range of communications capabilities as the profession-

> **SMART Marketing:**
>
> Mass marketing is becoming irrelevant in our fragmented society. It is difficult today to get anyone to admit to being a member of the "masses."

als. This has not only made our audiences more difficult to impress; it has diminished the opportunity for any one medium to hold the human attention span for more than the briefest second.

SMART conducted a proprietary survey of 933 respondents in the top 100 areas of dominant influence (ADIs) across America. This survey, which cut across cultural and economic strata, revealed that 83 percent of the respondents cited moderate to heavy monthly usage of 15 of the 17 media options we listed in the survey.

Consider your own environment. You are a consumer of everything you own, including this book. Ask yourself: How many of your purchases were influenced by television in the past year? How many by something you read? How many by something you were told by someone whose judgment you trust? No matter who you are, what you do to earn a living, or where you live, statistics indicate that fewer of your purchase decisions were influenced by television advertising than by something you read or something you were told. Our survey respondents indicated the same thing. Year after year, the persuasion scores of television commercials go down, even as the cost of production and television time rocket upward. Nevertheless, corporate America continues to shovel billions into the "mass market" on the advice of Madison Avenue and the so-called mass media.

At SMART, we employ economic, usage, affinity, cultural, and demographic segmentation criteria, which can reveal not only a market segment, but often subsegments as well. These selected consumers will give us the insight we need to position our clients' products or services to their sphere of influence. From that point on, we expand the product/service influence through ongoing relationship opportunities with our selected consumers. One impression at a time.

CASE STUDIES IN SELECTIVE MARKETING

What do people want? Ultimately, only the people themselves know. To give them what they want, then, marketers have to ask them. Mass marketing tells people what they want. Selective marketing asks people what they want. To be sure, asking requires more work. And different work. For the amount of money a mass-marketing campaign wastes on a network television campaign that reaches as many—if not more—nonprospects than prospects, a selective marketing campaign can establish an interactive relationship with thousands of affirmed prospective buyers, thereby all but guaranteeing a profitable return on investment.

Selective marketing is powerful, and in the case studies that make up the rest of this book, you will see that power at work.

In this book, you will discover how selective marketing was employed to

- Capture a new generation of customers for a high-end men's store on Rodeo Drive in Hollywood (Chapter 1).
- Reestablish the dominance of Johnson & Johnson's BAND-AID Brand Adhesive Bandages (Chapter 2).
- Disseminate life-saving information—and hope—to HIV+/ AIDS patients and, in the process, extend the market for a growing medical group (Chapter 3).
- Turn Drake's Cakes and Pastries from an also-ran to market leader (Chapter 4).
- Motivate two rival street gangs in Watts to end a 10-year war that had claimed 10,000 lives (Chapter 5).
- Carve a niche for Hardee's restaurants in an already crowded fast-food chicken market (Chapter 6).
- Convince a select group of marketing, merchandising, and manufacturing decision makers to license Turner Home Enter-

tainment's Hanna-Barbera animated characters for its branded and nonbranded products (Chapter 7).

- Put a halt to the "sibling" rivalry between the branches of a Los Angeles hotel chain and prevent them from depleting the market, by giving each a segment to target (Chapter 8).
- Broaden the market for Dr Pepper in a market previously dominated by Coca-Cola, 7UP, and Pepsi (Chapter 9).
- Demonstrate that a smaller medical center had advantages over larger, more well-known competitors in the area, thereby giving it greater market share (Chapter 10).
- Earn back the trust in government support by inner-city small businesspeople, whose lives and establishments were damaged or destroyed by race riots (Chapter 11).
- Prove that a communications giant—AT&T—understood and could accommodate the specific needs of individual market segments—in this case, the company's Hispanic customer base (Chapter 12).
- Revitalize customer interest in Kentucky Fried Chicken's bill of fare by acknowledging and addressing the *changing* tastes of one market segment and the *unchanging* tastes of a second market segment (Chapter 13).
- Regain the faith and trust of the Ford Motor Company's stockholders in the face of astounding losses (Chapter 14).
- Create an electronic "community in cyberspace" for the enthusiasts of Athearn Trains in Miniature.

MEASURE TWICE, CUT ONCE: HOW TO SELECT YOUR MARKET

Before diving into our case studies, you should know how to identify your target market. Once you have determined exactly which segments of the population are using your product or service, or are receptive to using your product or service, and which segments are not, you've got some measuring to do. The easiest place to start is with the numbers you have on hand—that is, current customers. Sort them by

Age	Memberships
Credit status	Military status
Economic status	Race
Education	Religion
Gender	Transportation (car owner, public transportation, bicycle, etc.)
Insurance status	
Job profile	Type of home (house, apartment, condominium, etc.)
Language	
Marital status	Zip code

or whatever other criteria are pertinent to the product or service that you have been hired to promote. All this information is available for a price—either of time or money. But if you can fill in 25 percent of the categories relevant to your targeted market for at least 1,500 of your client's current or prospective customers, you will have a *projectable sample,* usable clues as to who is and is not using the product or service you've been given the task of marketing. When you've gone as far as you can, sort them out.

Rank each customer in terms of the segment characteristics most prevalent in the group—whether it's more men, more women, more over 40 or under 30, more Hispanics, more skilled workers, and so on. This first tabulation will give you your first insight into who your market is (and isn't).

Next, re-sort those 1,500 by matching up all those with two, three, or four segment characteristics in common. If your first sort told you that more men than women buy the product or service, that's a beginning. If your two-trait sort found that most of the men were over 40, that gives you another piece of the puzzle. If your three-trait sort revealed that most of those 40-something men were Asian, you can begin to rule out more media outlets that would be a waste of time and money. If your four-trait sort tells you the vast majority of these Asian men live in upscale zip codes, you've narrowed the media field still further.

Now it's time to measure twice. Retab your two- and three-trait sorts to come up with a first, second, third, and fourth prototype segment subject. Put together four focus groups of users in ranks 1 to 4 and four focus groups of nonusers in ranks 1 to 4. Determine whether interest levels and product satisfaction levels are consistent between focus group users and the first 1,500 sample tabulations. If the outcome is significantly different between groups and tabs, set up a second group. If the second group's response to the product is consistent with that of the first focus group and inconsistent with initial tabulations, rethink designating this group as a selected market.

If, however, both focus group and customer data tabulations indicate strong product interest in your first, second, third, or fourth segment prospect, designate it an official selected market for your product or service and start doing your homework. Dig. Dig. Dig. Lurk. Lurk. Lurk.

Here's the process in a nutshell:

MEASURE

1. Start with 1,500 current customers.

2. Find out everything you can about them.

3. Sort your customers into segments based upon those factors you deem relevant to the product or service.

4. Note who the heavy, medium, and light users are.

5. Note which segments are missing from the sample.

6. Sort heavy, medium, and light users by matching traits.

7. Tabulate percentage of matching traits.

The largest category becomes the primary selected market; the smallest category becomes the secondary selected market.

CONFIRM

1. Organize focus groups of primary selected market and secondary selected market users and nonusers to confirm and augment or refute and clarify findings of the first 1,500 sample.

CUT

1. Enter the selected market armed with your research.

2. Be prepared to alter or modify your perceptions and the strategy and tactics of your selective marketing initiative as you gain ongoing knowledge about the placement of your product or service in the lives of those you seek to influence.

3. Create a collective experience for your product or service, to meet and/or exceed the expectations of the target market.

From these processes will come the feedback that selective marketers utilize in crafting each of the relationship opportunities embedded in the selective marketing initiative: precise media planning, compelling creative materials, interconnectivity with core consumers. As each segment begins to take shape in the selective marketing initiative, it's time to fine-tune the elements; then refine and redefine. All this effort is essential to set the stage for "the message."

This, then, is the intellectual capital we have at our disposal. We have their home addresses; we can mail them. We have their home telephone numbers; we can call them. We know the kind of cars they drive; we can use that to gain their attention. We have their media preferences; we can advertise to them. We have their food preferences; we can cross-promote to them. We know their ages; we can appeal to their sense of well-being. We know their educational backgrounds; we can establish rapport. We know their cultural backgrounds; we can build empathy. We know their genders; we can appeal to their fantasies. We know their economic status; we can anticipate price concerns. We know how they think; we can overcome their resistance. We know their needs, desires, and expectations; we can sell them.

Karen Richie, executive vice president for General Motors Mediaworks, wrote in her book, *Marketing to Generation X* (Lexington Books, 1995), "It is the next generation of media and marketing executives who must decide what to save and what to discard from today's disorganized heritage of conventional marketing techniques, radical think, and pop psychology. . . . The Boomer Era is ending fast." This transformation will be facilitated by the use of selective marketing initiatives from companies that have mastered the art of tailoring their clients' products or services. These companies will strive to meet the needs and expectations of those consumers with whom they share a meaningful relationship, and this book will show them and you exactly how to do it.

1

THE RODEO CIRCUIT:

Roping a High-End Select Market

for Battaglia Menswear

- **Market:** Next-generation affluent men with assets of $1 million or more, and their significant others.

- **Marketing Challenge:** Capture the next-generation replacements of an aging customer base.

- **Marketing Solution:** Use the cachet of the previous clientele to generate interest among the targeted select market of their younger counterparts.

- **Outcome:** The rebirth and resurgence to prominence of a proud retail men's clothing store.

R odeo Drive is host to the world's most expensive retailers and the most affluent shoppers. It is a high-ticket fantasia where money is no object and the mantra is: If you have to ask how much it costs, you can't afford it. There, Battaglia is, foot for foot of selling space, one of the most expensive menswear stores in the world. The premier salon for the Brioni line, the suits begin at $3,500 and go up to five figures. Shirts begin at $750, and two Stefeno Ricci ties can set you back a grand and change. Silk boxers at $125 are the least expensive clothing item in the salon. On entering, the customer sinks into the ultraplush carpeting.

Every footstep feels expensive. Rosewood display cases and walls of mirrors reflect the elegance of a bygone era. The aroma is of wealth and power. Battaglia's selected consumer is very select indeed.

Established by Dr. Giuseppe Battaglia, the man credited with introducing the classic Italian style to America, the store has been on Rodeo Drive for more than 30 years. Battaglia has been clothier to the most famous names in Hollywood, from Fred Astaire to Adolph Zukor, for more than a quarter of a century. But the source of the store's fame and fortune had become the cause of its concern. The old Hollywood was dying out, literally and figuratively. For the first time in its history, Battaglia realized that it was going to have to actively pursue new clientele if it was going to survive. The store brought in SMART to help do that.

When SMART opened for business in 1986, it was one of the first agencies to devote itself exclusively to the practice of selective marketing. Battaglia, Rodeo Drive, became its first client. Our initial step was to learn more about who Battaglia's current customers were. We began by monitoring the floor traffic. In four hours, only nine customers entered the store. However, the total sales for those nine customers was in excess of $38,000. But who were these people, and where could we find more of them?

LIFESTYLES OF THE RICH AND FAMOUS

The two most elusive audiences in America are at opposite ends of the consumer spectrum: the homeless and the megarich. But what they have in common is their primary mode of communication: word of mouth. Battaglia's—and hence, SMART's—target market, affluent men with assets of $1 million or more, could not be researched via the standard focus groups or mall intercepts. Millionaires don't do phone surveys, nor do they respond to questionnaires.

SMART had to find another way to track these elusive consumers. Fortunately, the answer was right at our feet, for Beverly Hills and its surrounding area have made the care and feeding of the rich, famous, and beautiful its raison d'etre. So first we identified 25 encounter points in Beverly Hills, Brentwood, Bel Air, and Malibu where the wealthy congregate. Places they wait for their cars to be brought to them. Places they dine. Places they have their nails manicured. Places they frequent after a rough turn on the polo field. We dispatched five handsome, well-dressed actors, each to an appropriate encounter point. They were instructed to small-talk their way into getting the answers to four questions SMART determined to be essential to profiling the select market.

> **SMART Marketing:**
>
> Retail outlets and product franchises that cater to exotic or specialized clientele must pursue new entrants to that customer base and not depend on word-of-mouth marketing.

Not only did we find out which age groups and professions had the highest levels of awareness of Battaglia, we found out why the new movers and shakers of Hollywood were passing the store by. As if protecting some small corner of their world that was being taken over by younger versions of themselves, the old guard in Hollywood wasn't sharing their sartorial secrets.

Our encounter-point interviews also revealed that older money and newer money have vastly different perceptions regarding what constitutes quality. Old money defines quality as something gained over years of experience and an intimate understanding of how things are made. New money trusts product claims of quality or relies on peer endorsements and style trends. To new money, quality is Armani, Versace, and Polo. To old money, it is Brioni and Saville Row. The question was: Could

> **SMART Marketing:**
>
> The more difficult a market segment is to reach and research, the more critical the information is to the selective marketing process.

SMART successfully interest new-money consumers in an old-money retailer?

Back for More

SMART initiated a second round of encounter-point surveys to find the answer to this all-important question. And the answer was what we and Battaglia hoped: Not only were members of the new Hollywood interested in learning from their predecessors, they were eager to learn.

Still we went back for more—four more times to be exact, before we believed we had enough insight into our targeted millionaires and their buying preferences. We also came to understand what Battaglia meant to the men who already shopped there. It had become an informal club of past and present "influentials" in the entertainment, energy, legal, medical, and financial fields. It was upon this concept-circle of influentials that we established the foundation on which to build our selective marketing strategy for bringing Battaglia into the next era.

> **SMART Marketing:**
>
> Never depend on one encounter with your selected market to give you the insight you need to reach it. Go back for more.

Secrets of the Rich and Famous

Our unorthodox research efforts made clear to us that our newly rich target audience believes the previous generation is holding back information about how the affluent live and how they judge quality. Thus, we devised the following strategy:

> Convince next-generation affluent men that there is a level of quality in men's furnishings that is above and beyond the level they currently perceive as best—specifically, a level of quality that can be obtained only at Battaglia, Rodeo Drive.

It was a daunting challenge.

GOING ONE STEP BEYOND THE BEST

While searching for the best approach to delivering better than the best, Battaglia's wise and urbane general manager, Alfred Chan, provided the agency with a dusty file full of photos from the 1950s and 1960s from Dr. Battaglia's archives. Each picture was more incredible than the previous one. There was a young Guiseppe Battaglia with Yul Brynner, Nat King Cole, Gary Cooper, Clark Gable—the big guys—taken at Hollywood social functions, Beverly Hills penthouse barbecues, summer homes in vacation spots all over the world. Still other photos showed these icons as they shopped at Battaglia's. Cooper buying a tie. Nat King Cole slipping into a vicuna coat. Billy Wilder being fitted for a tux.

Worth a Thousand Words

SMART's first recommendation was to enlarge the best of the photos of the stars shopping to 23-×-36 sepia-tone framed prints and display them prominently in the store, to bring Battaglia's glorious past into the present. Although this was only a cosmetic change at the point of sale, traffic made up of women shopping for their husbands and boyfriends did pick up—a fact SMART was quick to capitalize on, because often the key influencers for upmarket men are their upmarket significant others.

> **SMART Marketing:**
>
> When focusing on a select audience, don't overlook their significant others who might be shopping for the target market.

SMART recommended building upon the "better half" of Battaglia's target market by restaging the Battaglia designer fragrance Essenza Por Huomo. At the time, it sold for $55 per ounce. We convinced management to raise the price to $100 and to support the relaunch of the fragrance with selective marketing efforts directed toward the women intimates of our target men. Our advertisement headline said it all:

Battaglia Essenza. The one scent worth millions.

Run in the publications geared to new money, such as *Los Angeles Magazine,* the signature cologne positioned the signature shop on Rodeo Drive. People who were unaware of Battaglia or who were previously too intimidated to do more than window-shop there now had an excuse to enter the store. SMART was also well aware that often an entry-level product can engage an adjacent segment of a target market, which can later or concomitantly be developed for expansion.

The strategy worked. Women bought Essenza for their husbands or boyfriends, who subsequently came in for their refills. The new millionaires began to discover a new level of quality in men's furnishings—a level "one step beyond the best."

MINDSCAPE PAINTING

Once we had succeeded in positioning Battaglia as "one step beyond the best," it became imperative to distribute this message to additional print media that would reach those who could afford better than the best. Every select market has what SMART refers to as a *perceptual mindscape,* made up of decision-making references based upon shared group values, acquired data, and personal criteria. From this mindscape, all new information is noticed, filtered, evaluated, and embraced or discarded. The process can take years or moments, depending upon how, when, and where new information is presented.

Although *Los Angeles Magazine* boasted the largest number of upmarket men in its readership, more than two-thirds of its circulation was well below Battaglia's targeted income/net-worth levels—a lot of wasted readership to pay for. SMART searched for new publishing ventures that were also trying to reach this elusive market.

Reading Is Fundamental

In evaluating publications for possible positioning of print ads, our criterion was service. Could the publication provide information compelling to the upmarket male audience? Could the publication offer a service important or essential to our upmarket audience? After subjecting several publishers to such analysis, we settled on the house publication for the Equestrian Center's indoor polo season and a hardcover magazine called the *Gold Book,* which was distributed in the suites of the finest hotels in Beverly Hills, Century City, and Bel Air, as well as the capitals of Europe and Asia. (Upscale hotels proved to be an excellent entry point for additional national and international sales. It was a cost-effective way to initially expand a market without having to purchase media in multiple locations. Hotel publications also have a longer shelf life and high pass-along ratios. Furthermore, the placement of the book in high-upscale hotels served as an audience prequalifier, ensuring that the reader was in the demographic we had defined for our target customer.) The *Gold Book* afforded Battaglia the opportunity to begin to form a long-term, one-to-one relationship with national and international clientele.

SMART was not above using the considerable clout of Battaglia's media budget to influence the editorial policies of those publications that we decided met our service criterion. When a publication has a circulation of less than 1 million, we never accept the so-called separation of advertising and editorial, because, as everyone knows, advertisements pay the salaries of the editorial staffs of such publications. SMART never lets the publishers forget that.

Party Time

Once we had the editorial cooperation of our chosen media, SMART's next step was to create a yearlong calendar of store-based events to give the editorial departments Battaglia-related events to cover on a regular basis. This events calendar was given four pages in the *Gold Book*.

In the spring, we helped arrange for Dr. Battaglia to receive an award from the Italian government for his 30 years of service in promoting the classic Italian style of menswear in America. In the fall, we staged a celebrity charity fashion show featuring Patrick Wayne, Lalo Shifferin, Ricardo Montalban, and Larry Hagman, hosted by Battaglia's former stock boy, George Hamilton. Proceeds from the clothing sold during the show were donated to the American Cancer Society's Children's Fund. Sidney Poitier, Charles Bronson, and Sid Shinberg were just a few of the celebrities in attendance. The event was covered by CNN and NBC as well as *Women's Wear Daily, M,* and *Esquire.* The *Equestrian Center Polo Book* ran the photos for an entire season. But the most important aspect of the event was that it gave the new Hollywood a chance to rub shoulders with the old Hollywood in a venue where the torch could be graciously passed—which was, after all, SMART's marketing challenge.

Old-World Service via New-World Technology

To celebrate its 25th anniversary on Rodeo Drive, Battaglia unveiled a Brioni suit created by Alfred Chan. Needless to say, this was no ordinary garment; the suit was made of cashmere and featured 24-karat-gold pinstripes. The tag: $100,000. This was at the height of the go-go 1980s, and the suit was featured in articles in both the *Wall Street Journal* and *Barron's.* Six of the so-called one-of-a-kind suits were ordered.

By the end of the year (1987), Battaglia had again become the menswear store by which all others were judged. We had succeeded in capturing our select market: the new millionaires. SMART followed up by helping Battaglia design a computerized database of every customer that came in the store. This gave

Battaglia management and sales staff instant access to their customers' preferences, as well as to their complete size information for all garments and accessories. Once a customer was entered in the database, he could place an order from anywhere in the world and have it filled and shipped immediately. In addition, when Mr. Chan made his biannual buying trips to Milano, he could take up-to-the-minute data on which sizes to order.

This new customer satisfaction system gave the Battaglia sales staff the ability to develop in moments the kind of insight that had previously taken them years to acquire—and that the next-generation millionaires had come to expect in their high-tech lives. Investing in a computer tracking system also meant that as the volume of Battaglia's business increased, the perception of personalized service that made the store "one step beyond the best" did not have to be compromised.

Select Marketing Lessons

SMART's experience with Battaglia yields several valuable select marketing lessons:

- The more select an audience is, the more critical it is to find ways to accurately profile that audience. And that means being inventive and persistent.
- It's important to approach such consumers gingerly, because they are used to communicating among themselves and often rely on word-of-mouth information; thus they are less likely to be influenced by outside sources.
- When trying to build a bridge between established and new clientele, it is essential to bring them together in venues comfortable for both groups.
- Never focus so intently on a target consumer that you overlook a potential extended target consumer—in the case of Battaglia, the women in our target men's lives.

Finally, it is important to know when it is time to move on to a new strategy, to maintain the momentum gained from an initial success. During SMART's second year with Battaglia, we decided to withdraw all advertising and instead utilize the store's now extensive new customer database to convert to catalog-focused promotion activities.

2

STUCK ON YOU:

Reestablishing Brand Dominance

for Johnson & Johnson's BAND-AID Brand Adhesive Bandages

- **Market:** Mothers of children from 4 to 16 years old who feel guilty about not being able to prevent their children's minor injuries and therefore want to do their best to treat them.

- **Marketing Challenge:** Regain market share lost to a competitor by reestablishing faith in BAND-AID Brand Adhesive Bandages.

- **Marketing Solution:** Reinforce brand loyalty by demonstrating product performance.

- **Outcome:** BAND-AID Brand Adhesive Bandages captured an 87 percent share of the adhesive bandage market.

In the 1950s and 1960s, television was still a relatively new phenomenon to millions of American households. It was just as new for mass marketers, who had yet to discover its power of persuasion and learn how to use it to competitive advantage. Still, early entrants in the field of television advertising enjoyed unparalleled success; it seemed any product they promoted during the airing of a popular television program flew off the shelves. But as competition for this vast and rapidly expanding audience intensi-

fied, the differences between advertisers started to blur for viewers, meaning they had to become ever more inventive if their products were to stay in the minds of consumers at least as long as it
took them to drive to the store.

   Johnson & Johnson was just such a mass marketer. J&J representatives came to the 73-year-old marketing organization, Young
& Rubicam, for an image boost for BAND-AID Brand Adhesive
Bandages, then the company's best-known consumer product line.
J&J's nearest competitor had been making inroads into J&J's territory with its "Ouchless" brand adhesive strips, and it was Y&R's
challenge to stop the infiltration.

THE MOMMY TRACK

BAND-AID Brand Adhesive Bandages quickly became a show-
case account at the agency, and all the best creative teams wanted
to work on it. Y&R's innovative spirit was echoed by Johnson &
Johnson, which enthusiastically backed marketing experiments in
multicolor, stars-and-stripes, flesh-colored,
and, ultimately, Sheer Strip BAND-AID
Brand Adhesive Bandages. And to directly
counter Curad, Johnson & Johnson's bandages were also made "ouchless." The
commercials and campaigns for these
designs won awards, but they weren't winning the support of the person who mattered most: the target customer—in this
case, mothers of young children. An internal J&J segmentation study had indicated
that in most households, moms wash the dishes, bathe the children,
and in general carry out the "kiss and make it better" duties.

SMART Marketing:

A campaign may be
regarded as innovative
and award-worthy by
peers in the industry,
but it can never be
considered successful
until the target
customer makes it so by
buying the product.

The problem was that these mothers, J&J's target market, were becoming annoyed not only that their children were wearing these "designer" strips as ornaments, but, more important, that the brand was no longer taking its job seriously. Certainly, the new strips were cute and fun to wear, but in the new "ouchless" form, they no longer stayed on cuts and bruises long enough for them to heal properly. The new adhesive developed to prevent them from sticking to wounds went too far; simply, it didn't stick long enough—especially in water. J&J immediately made improvements to give superior performance in staying on and not hurting coming off.

EYE ON THE PRIZE

I had just begun working at Young & Rubicam when the call for the new BAND-AID Brand Adhesive Bandages campaign came down. At the same time that Y&R was gearing up to stanch bleeding sales of the bandage, Curad had been bought by Colgate-Palmolive, and we knew a marketing tour de force against BAND-AID Brand Adhesive Bandages was imminent. Y&R creative director Michael Becker gave me the opportunity of a lifetime, and I threw myself into the J&J product research, learning everything I could about "mass transfer," that white, sticky residue left on the skin after removing a bandage. I also lived day and night with consumer research, poring over the results of consumer panels, focus groups, and one-on-one mall intercepts that J&J's researches had conducted around the country. I even took it upon myself to visit every mother I knew in New York City. It didn't take long to isolate the problem: Consumer after consumer complained how disappointed they were when their bandages fell off—whether it happened while they were working or playing or bathing.

Emotional Intelligence

The insights we gained from analyzing the research enabled us to chip away at the mass-market monolith of BAND-AID Brand Adhesive Bandages and to begin to formulate a segmented—selected—market for the product. Selective marketing takes into account the cultural, professional, geographical, physical, chronological, and economic elements that define a prospective consumer; it then factors in the emotions of the prospective customer and how those emotions generate a common need. Selective marketing then determines how to touch the emotion that prompts consumers to purchase the product that will meet their need. Selective marketing, when used effectively, can establish long-term relationships between motivated buyers and the products they relate to.

> **SMART Marketing:**
>
> No meaningful campaign can be launched without a full understanding of the wants and needs of your selected market segment.

In the case of BAND-AID Brand Adhesive Bandages, the emotion we identified as most compelling to our target consumers (mothers of young children) was, simply, concern—concern that the product they were buying to protect and help heal their children's injuries be reliable. Their need, then, from this product was reassurance and confidence that it would work as promised.

Riding the Product Cycle

Selective marketing also requires that we be in tune with the targeted consumer's perceptions and preferences throughout the three-stage product cycle of (1) consider, (2) purchase, and (3) use. Riding this cycle successfully is a four-step process:

1. Determine the target consumer's need.
2. Make an emotional commitment to meet that need.
3. Identify the best route to take to meet the need.
4. Fulfill the need to the customer's satisfaction.

STAYING POWER

We had identified our product's problem (while becoming fashion-able, BAND-AID Brand Adhesive Bandages had let its old friends down by also becoming unreliable) and we had identified the target market whose loyalty and trust we had to regain (concerned mothers of young children). Johnson & Johnson was well on the way to solving the adhesive durability problem, so now all Young & Rubicam had to do was design a campaign to ensure the brand's dominance in the adhesive bandage market.

In the past, BAND-AID Brand commercials had been warm, fuzzy mini-melodramas about children and swings and kissing away the hurt, accented with the appropriate background music. Our client at J&J wanted something different.

Jingle Bells
During the research phase of the campaign development, one of the best local jingle houses in town had been trying to sell me on the idea of using jingles. As a veteran of Motown Records, I was resistant. But one day, with one of the aforementioned visuals prominent in my mind, Tommy Hamm, the rep from the jingle house called again. The timing was right. I had been thinking about something one of "my" mothers had told me: "I used to be stuck on them until they started falling off in the dishwater." From there, I began to think about people singing in the shower, and the beginnings of a theme came to me: They are stuck on their Band-Aid 'cause their Band-Aid is stuck on them. I couldn't let go of the idea, and I worked out more of the words to the jingle:

I'm stuck on Band-Aid 'cause Band-Aid's stuck on me.
'Cause they hold on tight in the bathtub
And they cling in soapy suds.
I'm stuck on Band-Aid 'cause Band-Aid's stuck on me.

I wrote this on the back of two business cards while in a cab driving through Central Park. Michael Becker polished the copy and all that was needed now was a great melodic hook.

Divine Providence

That night I had plans to go with a friend to a cabaret show that had become all the rage in New York's fashion underground. The star of the show was a brassy, buxom redhead who was billed as "The Divine Miss M." And, indeed, Bette Midler did bring the house down, but consumed as I was with the J&J campaign, I was more impressed with her accompanist, so my friend got me the piano player's name before we left. The next morning, Barry Manilow sat down at the piano and the two of us pieced together a memorable 30 seconds of words and music.

> **SMART Marketing:**
>
> Nothing is more memorable to an audience than music; therefore, nothing is more detrimental to a campaign than using the wrong music.

Telling the Story

To tell a story that would sell the new image of BAND-AID Brand Adhesive Bandages, Mike Becker and I combined two issues. First, both of us had been concerned about the absence of multiculturalism in commercials, and a breakdown of sales penetration by zip code had shown that African Americans, Asians, rural whites, teens, and working women were key consumer franchises, yet no advertising for the brand had ever been directly addressed to these segments of the population. Second, I had become intrigued by a then new filmic technique called the *vignette,* in which, instead of telling one story in 30 seconds, an art director could tell many stories in the same amount of time. These two concepts began to suggest some visuals. For example:

Scene: An Asian boy in the bathtub with his rubber ducky. He climbs out of the tub, and does his best imitation of a karate chop—

demonstrating clearly that the bandage on his hand stayed on in water.

Together with painstakingly designed full-color storyboards, a catchy jingle, and music by Barry Manilow, the campaign met with the enthusiasm of creative head Alex Kroll and was presented to Johnson & Johnson, where it met with almost universal approval. Only the J&J legal department had a concern: They insisted that the first line of the jingle had to be changed to "I'm stuck on BAND-AID *Brand Adhesive Bandages.*" Quite a mouthful. J&J was determined that its brand and trademark would not slip into public domain status through common use, as had Jell-O and Kleenex. It took us four months to convince J&J that singing "I'm stuck on BAND-AID Brand . . ." just once in the jingle would be sufficient.

Once the client approved the campaign, Y&R producer Phylis Landi and commercial director Bob Giraldi set about bringing the campaign to life. For that we cast a series of unknowns that included Terri Garr and John Travolta in their singing debuts.

BRANDED

To say that the campaign was a smash hit would be an understatement. The campaign won a place in the Clio Hall of Fame in 1991. How did it do in the marketplace? Mike Becker, who is now chief creative officer for the Wunderman Cato Johnson arm of Young & Rubicam, mentioned that former client Gerald M. Ostrov, Company Group Chairman, is still heading up BAND-AID Brand Adhesive Bandages for J&J Consumer Products. In 1997, Mr. Ostrov asked for a new campaign from current agency McCann-Erickson. They brilliantly adapted the "Stuck on Me" commercial to benefit from the brand/advertising and message awareness of the past and communicated the news of the breakthrough antibiotic BAND-AID

Brand product. According to Mr. Ostrov, "Stuck on Me" is a great campaign because it embodies all of the positive attributes of the brand in a simple, coherent message, delivered visually, verbally, and musically. Obviously, this campaign has hit a nerve in our selected segment of concerned moms then as well as now. They seem to be stuck on it.

Select Marketing Lessons

An important lesson to be gleaned from Y&R's work with Johnson & Johnson's Band-Aid Brand is that for products that provide a service, especially a safety- or health-related service, function is more important than form. While it is well and good to have fun with the design of a product, if it doesn't also carry out its function reliably, consumers will go elsewhere. A Band-Aid that doesn't stick, no matter how innovatively designed, will not sell. And selective marketing techniques are valuable for identifying such issues. For example, J&J's research of the primary adhesive bandage buyer—mothers of young children—helped us to quickly isolate the cause of Band-Aid Brand's slipping sales.

Selective marketing can also point the way to the most effective way to promote a product. Again using research—in this case, sales breakdowns by zip code—we were able to isolate those groups most needful of direct interaction and thus most likely to respond to a campaign. By choosing to use a diverse group of vignettes featuring a variety of ethnic and cultural segments of the population, we were able to tap select markets heretofore ignored.

Finally, it is important to remember that sometimes the best way to make a serious point is with a lighthearted approach and with timeless words and music. Music is the universal language, and well-written words in combination with a catchy tune have a long shelf life. "Stuck on Band-Aid Brand . . ." was so successful that the campaign was resurrected in the mid-1980s and again in the early 1990s to become one of the longest-running ad campaigns on television.

3

MEDICAL MARKETING:

Providing Information— and Hope—

for Pacific Oaks Medical Group

- **Market:** Men and women diagnosed as HIV positive or with AIDS.

- **Marketing Challenge:** Inform HIV+/AIDS patients of new therapies and treatments that might improve their prognosis and extend their lives.

- **Marketing Solution:** Implement a national question-and-answer forum for disseminating this important information. Position Pacific Oaks Medical Group as the practice setting the standards in HIV/AIDS medical care and treatment.

- **Outcome:** The client, Pacific Oaks Medical Group, grew from 9 to 16 doctors and is currently the largest private HIV+/AIDS medical practice in America.

The AIDS virus was first isolated by a group of Los Angeles doctors affiliated with the University of California at Los Angeles (UCLA) in 1981. Later that year, one of those early pioneers, Joel D. Weisman, D.O., along with a colleague from Sherman Oaks, Eugene H. Rogolsky, M.D., founded the Pacific

Oaks Medical Group. Over the years, they were joined by several young doctors whose practices were being decimated by this viral scourge. Together, they began to focus their efforts on the care and treatment of those diagnosed as HIV positive or living with AIDS.

Consequently, Pacific Oaks is not just another Beverly Hills medical group. Its staff is at the leading edge of HIV/AIDS medicine in America. Because its doctors treat patients from all over the country, Pacific Oaks is the closest thing this country has to a national medical group for HIV medicine. However, as it began to grow, the group feared it was running the risk of being perceived as the General Motors of HIV/AIDS medicine; that is, staff members were concerned they would be regarded as running an assembly-line practice. Consequently, Pacific Oaks chose to launch an outreach program with the objective of informing the HIV+/AIDS population of the scope of its services and treatment options.

SMART was awarded the Pacific Oaks Medical Group's Patient Outreach Campaign. At the time, my knowledge of HIV/AIDS boiled down to this: If you had it, you would die. I also realized that if ever there was a selective market about which it was essential to become thoroughly informed, this was it.

WHOSE LIFE IS IT ANYWAY?

We at SMART began the difficult process of gaining insight into the mind-set of HIV+/AIDS patients. Out of respect for the privacy of these patients and the almost incomprehensible difficulty of the decisions they were facing, it was imperative that we find the right way to seek and gain true understanding of our select market. Clearly, SMART had to take an emotional rather than a clinical approach. With input from the nine doctors then in practice at

Pacific Oaks, and under the direction of R. Scott Hitt, M.D., a partner in the practice and chairman of the White House Task Force on HIV/AIDS, we began to develop the practice's first selective marketing program.

Through interviews with patients, we attempted to identify everything our selected consumers cared about as well as the keys to their decision-making processes regarding treatment. Through a series of focus groups conducted with men and women who were living with HIV/AIDS, we began the search for answers. Respondents were recruited by posting notices at pharmacies that specialized in HIV/AIDS treatments and through recruitment at AIDS service organizations. Questionnaires were developed jointly by the doctors at Pacific Oaks and the SMART research staff. The groups were moderated by a psychotherapeutic professional; some of the doctors participated as observers, while others were content to read the study results after they were compiled. Defining and analyzing the HIV+/AIDS population proved to be a balancing act of assuring absolute confidentiality and anonymity, while delving into intimate details of individual lives. But if the selective marketing program was to have any chance of success, we had to acquire specific, rather than general, knowledge of the mindset of our consumers.

> **SMART Marketing:**
>
> The difference between popular opinion and applicable experience can mean the difference between success and failure in issues-based campaigns.

Understandably, most people diagnosed as HIV positive or living with AIDS battle apathy and depression every day. We learned there were two seemingly opposite ways people fight these demons. Some patients use information as their weapon; they constantly seek news—any news—about their condition; about research; about drugs, therapies, and treatments. Others try to ignore or deny their condition as long as they possibly can. Each of these attitudes posed specific problems for the Pacific Oaks team at SMART.

We learned that the challenge posed by the consumers who were voraciously devouring any and all medical information was that, typically, they were apathetic to information they could not apply in their lives immediately; therefore, complex messages could get lost. We had to find a way to make a memorable impression if our selective marketing program was to achieve its goal. For those consumers in denial, the challenge, obviously, was to engage them in our campaign in the first place. Our study showed that those consumers who were in denial about their HIV-positive status responded best when assured of understanding and supportive caregivers.

> **SMART Marketing:**
>
> When employing selective marketing techniques, assume the target customers know more than you do about the service or product. Then find a way to get them to share that information with you.

SPIN DOCTOR

Medical marketing has a bad reputation. It is the one area of promotion that makes everybody, doctors and patients alike, uncomfortable at best and repels them at worst. Many physicians feel that advertising their skills and/or practice is somehow demeaning, and much of the public regards doctors who advertise as less than competent (otherwise why would they have to advertise for patients?)—and no one wants an incompetent taking care of them. Understandably, the HIV+/AIDS population is the most wary of all.

> **SMART Marketing:**
>
> Once a population segment gains its own voice and media infrastructure, it becomes a market segment, with the ability to become a selected market.

SMART's research validated that attitude. Respondents were adamant about taking charge of their treatment, and they did not want to see themselves portrayed as victims or poster children for medical advertising. A typical criticism of our early creative efforts shown to focus groups was: "Don't give us ads, dammit. Give us a cure." The SMART team learned from those failed attempts that we had to find a way to use understanding as the key strategic element, supported by knowledge.

So we held more focus groups, to gain deeper insight into the self-image of our selected consumers. We listened to—and heard—their point: "We're not straight or gay anymore. We are people living with AIDS." That gave SMART the focus we needed to fine-tune each element of the Pacific Oaks selective marketing program to the hearts and minds of our selected consumers.

For the Public Good

To succeed, we had to juxtapose our need to understand our consumers with our need for our consumers to understand Pacific Oaks's message. On behalf of Pacific Oaks, we had to communicate in a meaningful way that the doctors and staff there truly understood the impact of being diagnosed as HIV positive or living with AIDS on a person's life, outlook, state of health and mind. Failure was not an option.

In the process of perfecting this campaign, we came to understand the fear, power, and politics that surround this dreaded disease. We recognized that the caliber of the work would have to preclude the impression that advertising on the part of Pacific Oaks was self-aggrandizement. It was unacceptable to the Pacific Oaks staff to be perceived as marketing their expertise in AIDS medicine. The campaign had to be viewed as a public-service effort.

> **SMART Marketing:**
>
> Health-related marketing demands understanding the emotions of the selected consumers. A lack of understanding can destroy your credibility, as well as the effectiveness of your message.

The SMART strategy was to embrace our selected audience with advertising, not sell them. To achieve that goal, SMART's media people recommended a national advertising plan. They believed there would be strong nationwide support for a group with the stature of Pacific Oaks. As one person put it, "If you live in Duluth and are diagnosed as HIV+, who you gonna call?" The first year, the campaign ran in monthly news and feature magazines with a primarily gay male readership. These publications included *The Advocate, Genre,* and *Out,* with a combined national circuulation of approximately 250,000. By utilizing these magazines, we were able to target at-risk populations in New York, Boston, Washington, D.C., Atlanta, Chicago, St. Louis, Denver, Salt Lake City, Dallas, San Francisco, and Seattle. Ads were also run in primarily gay-focused publications in Los Angeles, Long Beach, Newport Beach, and Palm Springs, and on billboards in the predominantly gay areas of Los Angeles.

The two-page, four-color spreads that SMART created for Pacific Oaks were more art than advertising; the copy was compelling and hopeful, and the tone was supportive. One ad showed a mother and father with their grown daughter and her husband preparing to leave on a hot air balloon ride, when their son appears and grasps his mother's hand. She looks in his eyes. As Dad looks skyward, the camera freezes the moment. The headline asked, "How Do You Tell Them You're HIV+?"

This first phase of the campaign was launched to create a feeling of empathy with our selected market. Since many of the Pacific Oaks doctors and staff were active in the gay and lesbian communities as well as supportive of HIV/AIDS causes, we used the campaign theme "Family Treating Family" to communicate the community-involved nature of Pacific Oaks. In addition to the family-oriented ad previously described, we ran ads that stated: "You Are Not Alone," "If You Look So Good, Why Do You Feel So Bad?," "You Take Better Care of Your Car Than Yourself," and "Beauty's More Than Skin Deep." Each of these ads urged readers to take an active part in maintaining their health and well-being and stressed the experience and supportive nature of the doctors and staff of Pacific Oaks.

The second phase of our selective marketing effort came about after one year of the "Family Treating Family" campaign. Again we went back to respondents from our targeted consumer group. This time we tested our first campaign to determine whether we should extend it or modify it. Overall, the majority of research participants reacted positively to the "Family Treating Family" campaign. They liked the images in the ads and reacted better to those ads that utilized full color because they found them to be more "uplifting," conveying hope and possibilities. Black-and-white ads were looked at as depressing. We determined that, although this campaign was not perceived as negative, it was still "quiet" when compared to the problem it was seeking to address.

Another round of focus groups inspired us to provide more cutting-edge information about the latest treatments and therapies. This time the respondents claimed we were giving them something. In the new campaign, we asked the doctors for their most-asked questions along with the most up-to-date medical answers. This information was used as a border treatment, while the center of the double-page spreads showed people engaged in outdoor activities. Each ad featured a positive, uplifting headline, such as: "HIV Care in America. We Set a Higher Standard Every Day," "People with HIV Are Living Longer," and "You Can Be Healthy and Still Be HIV+." Our new theme line was "Setting the Standard for HIV Care in America," which was a clear, concise statement of truth.

LEADING BY FOLLOWING

After two years of emotional, informative, and powerful selective marketing strategies, the Pacific Oaks Medical Group doubled in size and currently has offices throughout Los Angeles and Orange

Counties. As of this writing, a Pacific Oaks physician, Dr. R. Scott Hilt, heads the White House AIDS initiative. Throughout Los Angeles today is a comprehensive network of medical practitioners who treat HIV-positive patients, large, well-funded AIDS service organizations, and committed government and private medical facilities. This constitutes the best continuum of HIV/AIDS care and treatment in the nation.

As a result of our work with Pacific Oaks, SMART was asked to author a compendium on the Los Angeles model for HIV/AIDS care for the White House. Thanks to our relationship with physicians and staff at Pacific Oaks and the Southern California Immune Suppression Unit of Midway Hospital Medical Center, we were able to deliver that important document.

Select Marketing Lessons

Medical marketing is without a doubt one of the most difficult challenges in the field. Applying selective marketing techniques can prove invaluable. When you apply mass-market communication skills together with selective market insights to targeted media, you can dominate the editorial environment; in short, you get noticed. The following are essential lessons to keep in mind before launching any campaign directed to a select market comprising consumers concerned with health-related issues.

- Before engaging your selected market head on, gain understanding of sensitive social or medical issues through collaboration with experienced practitioners who have proven themselves in your selected market segment. In the medical field, doctors and their professional organizations and charitable associations are avenues to pursue; pharmaceutical companies can also be very helpful.

- The characteristics of illness are more important to certain selected consumers than any cultural, societal, or political delineations. Therefore, when beginning the work of identifying and analyzing your target consumers, remember that phone polls and surveys cannot reveal the information you seek with the depth and accuracy of focused discussion groups and personal interviews.

- Successful medical marketing is dependent on quality of information: It tells the patients and their loved ones what to talk about and how to talk about it. It should not be perceived by the selected market as a direct sell of a drug, treatment, or practitioner.

4

LET 'EM EAT DRAKE'S:
Getting the (Baked) Goods on the Competition
for Borden's Drake's Bakeries

- **Market:** New York City's uptown kids.

- **Marketing Challenge:** Capture the all-important New York section of the Northeast Corridor market from an entrenched competitor.

- **Marketing Solution:** Utilize the selected consumers to sell their peer group.

- **Outcome:** Drake's cakes and fruit pies succeeded in dominating the market.

The so-called Northeast Corridor represents almost half of the nation's baked goods business, a market worth $340 million in 1978. After being acquired by Borden's, Drake's Bakeries had the deep pockets that enabled the company to make a legitimate bid for that lucrative market. Its competition? None other than Continental Bakeries, purveyor of the Hostess brand, makers of Twinkies and the chocolate cupcakes (with the surprise inside). Not inconsequentially, also vying for the same piece of the pie (pun intended) was Sunshine Bakers and dozens of mom-and-pop brands.

In the Northeast Corridor, key to success was the Big Apple, New York City, and as the song says, "If you can make it there, you can make it anywhere." Drake's agreed, and hired Needham, Harper Steers, where I was then working as an executive art director to capture that very tough—and expensive—market. Several of the firm's creative teams were put on the project.

THE WAY THE COOKIE CRUMBLES

By scanning the Drake's zip code–indexed sales data, we were able to quantify what the Drake's sales force had been saying but that other creative teams had ignored: New York's "uptown" demographic was primarily African American and Hispanic (Puerto Rican and Dominican), which indexed at four times the area norm, with two-thirds of the business concentrated in one-third of the New York, New Jersey, and Connecticut metropolitan area. If Drake's could dominate the uptown snack market, it would own New York City in sales volume.

> **SMART Marketing:**
>
> Selling by segment enables the use of more efficient targeted media, and precludes the cost—and waste—of more general outlets.

This was not going to be easy, because in store check after store check we had seen our consumers fork over their lunch money for the competitor's yellow "puff dogs," while our client's delicious chocolate Yodels sat untouched in their neatly stacked boxes. It was as if they were invisible.

It didn't take market research to tell us that our target customers weren't passing up our client's product because of its ingredients or nutritional requirements—they didn't care about such things. Pure and simple, it was because they didn't know anything about Drake's products; consequently, Drake's had zero share of "mind awareness" among our selected market. (At the time,

> **SMART Marketing:**
>
> Just showing up on the shelf is not enough to build a brand preference. Absence of information about it in the media categorizes it as a "so what" brand.

Drake's advertised only on Saturday morning television, and the company's commercials were lost in a jungle of messages that were more important to the viewers in that day-part.)

In contrast, Hostess cupcakes were "in their face" every day after school on *American Bandstand*—at the time, one of the most popular television shows in that time slot. Clearly, Hostess knew what Drake's was just beginning to learn. *American Bandstand* was the essence of selective marketing to the teen and 'tween (8- to 12-year-olds) segments of the mass market. Hostess had chosen to market selectively and, as a result, had captured the market.

Using Consumers to Sell Themselves

Sounded like a job for selective marketing, which is what my team recommended to the client. Once the account group and the client bought off on the efficiencies and reach that could be afforded by the use of selective marketing, the next step was to sell them on our creative strategy, which was to capture the loyalty of New York's uptown kids and let *them* sell Drake's to their peers.

Other teams at Needham had pitched campaigns featuring everything from superheros to dancing cupcakes. My team believed that the kids in our target audience knew far better than we did what would motivate their peers to take notice of Drake's. The client agreed, and all systems were go to test the concepts behind selective marketing, in a very competitive arena.

A Failure to Communicate Is a Failure to Sell

In the marketing profession, the definition of communication that I prefer is: "the art and science of moving a clear message from one point to another." The art is in the *method* we choose to communicate; the science is the *means* by which we choose to employ that method. Add marketing to the mix, with its sibling terms "product" and "service," and the definition becomes: "the art and science of moving a clear product or service message from one point to another." Selective marketing adds the adjective "efficiently" to "moving," "relevant" to "clear," and "specific" to "point." Finally, the definition of selective marketing communication is: "the art and science of efficiently moving a clearly relevant product or service message from one specific point to another."

This definition fit our vision of the new Drake's campaign to a T, for we had decided to use "kidvertising," that is, advertising *from* uptown kids *to* uptown kids. Larry Spector, Needham vice president, and I spent a lot of our development time learning the language and customs of the kids we were trying to influence. We called it gaining "insider smarts." To succeed in this endeavor, we had to put aside all our preconceived notions about our target audience and silence any dismay we may have felt for their music, their clothing, their street talk. Simply put, before we could put our selective marketing principles to work, we had to become intimately familiar with the target consumer. If music was going to play an important role in our selective marketing program, we had to learn about the music of the selected market. If it was sports, we had to find out which sport and then find out who the players were. It didn't matter if we, personally, didn't like rap or preferred baseball to basketball—what mattered was that we became interested and knowledgeable in whatever our selected customers were interested in and knowledgeable about.

> **SMART Marketing:**
>
> Once you establish a line of communication with your target market, keep it open. Conditions within a segment change continually, and your selective marketing efforts have to reflect those changes to remain effective.

With our insider information in hand, Larry and I then worked on a basic framework and timing for 30-second television and 60-second radio spots. At the same time, working with the Needham media department and several community-based organizations, we set up a 500-diary "uptown Nielsen's" system to start generating feedback on the television habits of our targeted uptown kids. That is to say that we made up

500 loose-leaf binders with two weeks' worth of daily pages that listed the time periods from 3:30 P.M. until 11 P.M. We then packed up the binders and four cases of Drake's products and shipped them to the Parent-Teacher Association of P.S. 211 in the Bronx for distribution among their membership. The PTA members and teachers made sure the children recorded their viewing habits faithfully every day. After two weeks, we visited the school, picked up the diaries, and sent them

> **SMART Marketing:**
>
> Don't even think of working in urban areas without the help and guidance of community groups and organizations.

to ASPIRA, a community-based organization in the same area, for tabulation by the group's data processing training program. Three weeks after we shipped out our 500 diaries, we had a ten-page document on the viewing habits of a representative sample of our selected market. We also began setting up casting sessions to recruit what we were calling our "uptown teen creative teams."

TAKING IT TO THE STREETS

Under the auspices of several grassroots social service agencies and organizations, we designed and distributed flyers by the thousands in both English and Spanish. They read, in part:

> Send us your Drake's commercial.
> You might get on TV.
> See your local store for details.

The retailers that carried Drake's in turn gave out a list of the community organizations processing our young hopefuls. Those retailers that didn't carry Drake's soon began calling the bakery after the fourth or fifth kid ran across the street to a competitor. The campaign was already working!

The response to the flyers was overwhelming, as was our subsequent effort to ensure that we gave every kid who came forward a fair shot. And they came in droves, along with parents, teachers, and counselors, all of whom gave us further insight into what made our targets tick. They also helped us to see more definitely how we could best move our message out of our Third Avenue, 14th-floor, ivory-tower offices and onto the streets of New York's uptown kids.

We culled the hundreds and hundreds of submissions we collected to 30 commercially workable ideas. We then presented those 30 ideas to focus groups composed of members of our target audience; we met variously in community spaces, private homes, even on neighborhood street corners. From those groups, four ideas emerged.

MIX AND MATCH

By the time we got those four ideas through the system, however, our target market had already begun to shift its style. The kids who were watching *American Bandstand* in 1978 were starting to shift their viewing habits to the more urban music–based *Jocko's Rocket Ship Show* and a syndicated show from Chicago called *Soul Train* by 1979 when the campaign broke. During the six months we were in campaign development, we began to notice distinct trend shifts in what our selected market was wearing, the music they were listening to, and the food they were eating. Low-priced, quick-service restaurants began cutting into our targets' lunch money allocations.

We learned all of this by keeping our research channels open during the creative and production phases of the campaign. Music that had been skewed toward Cuban/Puerto Rican salsa rhythms had to be expanded to accommodate the huge influx of merengue-loving Dominican teens migrating into the New York metro area. Wardrobe had to be changed to accommodate the more stylish outfits introduced by the *Soul Train* dancers and growing dance club movement. Once we told our community-based partners the kinds of information we were after, we found ourselves being invited to cultural events, neighborhood socials, and talent contests—all in the spirit of keeping us up on what was hot and what was not. Our great lesson in this campaign was to keep our strategy loose enough to accommodate the constant change that was indicative of our selected market's early-adapter lifestyle and value structure.

> **SMART Marketing:**
>
> The target market is also a moving target. To be effective, marketers not only have to get in touch, they have to stay in touch.

When Alex Ramos came for his audition, the client and the agency agreed to bend the rules we had set for the campaign from using only teen-generated concepts to include a great spokesperson who could transcend the trends in music and fashion by virtue of his or her own personal magnetism and charisma. Although Alex's own idea for a commercial to sell Drake's cakes and pies was not a winner, *he* was. His personality lit up the screen on his audition tape. Everyone who saw the tape loved him. He was handsome, dynamic, and engaging. So, we decided to keep Alex but come up with a better idea and put them together, in what amounted to a mix-and-match strategy.

The better idea came on the final day of our open casting calls. It was a Saturday, and 15 kids and their friends and families showed up at the gym in P.S. 112 in the Bronx. The vocal category winner was a no-brainer: Nate Smith, of Manhattan—who claimed to be related to singer Nancy Wilson—stood up with his group and sang, a cappella, their doo-wop salute to Drake's fruit pies:

Drake's fruit pies
Make me feel so fly.
They come in apple and cherry.
Give each one a try.

They brought the house down. We had not intended this probe for campaign concepts from our selected market to turn into a neighborhood talent contest, but it did. Initially, we thought it would be neat to take one of the many reworked pop songs that we got as contest entries and get the original recording artist to sing it in a neighborhood location surrounded by local fans—much the way the Beatles' famous London rooftop performance was filmed. Nate Smith's a capella group scrapped that idea. Ultimately, we put Nate and his backup singers on the front stoop of an uptown brownstone. Director Steve Horn shot them live, with Nate's strong tenor voice and his friends' four-part harmony cutting through the ambient traffic noise to make a terrific 30-second performance.

Back to the open casting call: With the applause for Nate still ringing in our ears, the gym doors slammed open and a handful of tough-looking teens walked in. Turned out they were members of the dreaded Savage Skulls, an infamous Bronx street gang. Their leader strode onto the makeshift stage and stilled the crowd with one look. He took out a piece of paper and read a poorly written ode to Drake's Yodels. When he was finished, he looked around the room, then directly at me, and said, "Pretty good, huh?"

He left as quickly as he came in, with his homeboys trailing behind him. As the gym erupted in nervous chatter, I had a brainstorm for a powerful spot: Substitute Alex Ramos for the gang leader in a commercial that reproduced the incident that had just occurred.

And that's what we did, complete with Alex standing in front of an auditorium full of silent kids, to whom he shouts, "Everybody Yodel!" Once again, director Steve Horn did a magnificent job of bringing the uptown kids' vision to the screen for Drake's. The campaign was so successful that Drake's went on to dominate the baked goods category in the Northeast through the early 1980s, when the brand again changed ownership. The television commercials were supported by transit posters, radio spots on both African-American and Latino stations, and point-of-sale materials that featured the winners and their ideas.

By the way, Alex Ramos became an aeronautical engineer, his college education financed by his talent payments from the Drake's campaign.

Select Marketing Lessons

The development of what we call *insider smarts*, which is essential to the success of any selective marketing program, has to start in your head. Rule number one, as we learned early in the Drake's campaign, is that you have to suspend personal tastes and value systems if you are to successfully understand those of your selected market. This can be a very difficult task when your audience and you seemingly have nothing in common. You may, for example, hate rap music, but if your selected market identifies with rap, you had better know the difference between Tupac, Ice Cube, and Puff Daddy.

Here are some hints for breaking through:

- Gain some starter information by reading topic-relevant magazines.

- Consider interviewing the writers of such publications; chances are, they already have made personal contact with members of your target group.

- Hire writers or other insiders as consultants. Find out from them which products and services your selected market prefers. Identify leaders of those industries if you have to, and talk to them.

- Attend seminars and trade shows; they provide ideal opportunities to meet and greet. Pump attendees for their opinions on the topics you've determined are important to your market.

- Finally, take to the streets. No secondhand information should ever be considered good enough to a selective marketer. Once you have background information, go after firsthand input. And don't forget to include in this group any key influencers of your target audience. In the Drake's campaign, we would have been lost without the influence of our kids' parents, teachers, counselors, and the community organizations.

5

MARKETING PEACE:

The Selling of an Idea

*for the Los Angeles City
Attorney's Office*

- **Market:** Los Angeles gang member affiliates.

- **Marketing Challenge:** Sell peace to warring gang members.

- **Marketing Solution:** Enlist gang members to communicate the benefits of peace in a medium that would both reach and influence peers.

- **Outcome:** Signing of a formal truce.

It was 1988 in Los Angeles, California, and in the previous eight years, approximately 10,000 people had been killed in gang-related homicides in L.A. County. Alarmingly, most L.A. residents were unaware of this war. And according to the city attorney's office, the age of the gang members was getting younger and younger. Indeed, 11- and 12-year-olds had been apprehended with 9mm Glocks and AK-47s loaded with chrome stocks and armor-piercing ammo. Within a four-mile area, two rival gangs had become involved in a brutal street war that was claiming more than 300 lives a year.

Tracy Robinson of the Gang Prosecution Unit of the Los Angeles City Attorney's Office asked SMART to help them communi-

cate with the 50,000-plus active members of the Crips (acronym
for "Continuing Revolution in Progress") and Bloods (for "Better
Look Out or Die") street gangs; specifically, Tracy wanted
SMART to find a way to help the unit reach out to the tens of thousands of young people that law enforcement refers to as "gang-
affiliated" youth (our market). The LAPD estimated that this
number represented one of every three African-American teens in
Los Angeles County. To understand the enormity of the challenge,
consider that there were 135,000 active Crips and Bloods, compared to 3,500 police officers in 1988.

THE WAR OUTSIDE

As the president of a Wilshire Boulevard advertising agency
whose clients represented the most prestigious names in Beverly
Hills, I was lost. I had not come in contact with the kids growing
up in the gang-dominated archipelago that makes up the Los
Angeles Unified School District in my four years as a resident or
my 30 years of production visits. I knew that if SMART accepted
the city attorney's proposal (pro bono, of course), as with any
selected market, we would have to immerse ourselves in the culture of the gangs before we could attempt to influence their behavior—that is, to sell them the idea of peace.

The more I learned, the more I felt like running as far away from
this marketing challenge as my credit cards would take me. I continued to put off accepting the challenge until one day I saw a TV
news report of a gang-related homicide at Fairfax High, where my
16-year-old son was going to school. I called Tracy at home and
signed up SMART for the duration.

IDEA AS PRODUCT

Going in, the SMART premise was that an idea could be sold like a product. In this case, the product was peace. And everything we knew about using selective marketing effectively led us to one conclusion: *The only ones who could stop the war were the gangs themselves.* SMART's first step, I knew, had to be to get the attention of the gangs' leadership long enough to motivate them into recognizing this fact, wanting it to happen, and then starting to act on it. Easier said than done. This was not a popularly held point of view among law enforcement or criminal justice professionals. To the contrary, the LAPD had named its gang unit C.R.A.S.H. (Community Response Against Street Hoodlums), which at one point had taken a tank onto the crime-ridden streets to demonstrate its intentions. The result? The gangs laughed at the tank and, for good measure, stole the computers out of the LAPD's black-and-whites.

SMART Marketing:

An idea can be sold like a product.

Needless to say, I didn't feel on firm ground. But Tracy Robinson was a rising star in City Attorney James Hahn's inner circle of political operatives. He had joined the Hahn camp from the Mondale presidential campaign and was now the office's liaison with the African-American community in Los Angeles. When I told him I thought the gangs themselves could be motivated to stop the war by selling them on the idea of peace, I could see the wheels turn in his head. He agreed to arrange for me to meet some gang members at a media event taking place in the Nickerson Gardens Gym in the heart of Watts by Hahn's father, County Supervisor Kenneth Hahn, who had been in office for 48 years. Hahn had the trust of local community leaders as well as the clout of the local Democratic Party power brokers who could deliver a national figure with the sizzle it would take to bring people out of their homes in this crime-ridden war zone. The sizzle was delivered by presidential candidate Jesse Jackson, who intended to spend the preceding night in the most unsavory housing project in America, then hold a "gang summit" the next morning.

That morning, standing in the gym that was crawling with plainclothes police and the press, Tracy directed my attention high in the rafters, where 8- and 9-year-old wannabes of the Bounty Hunter Blood Gang were watching us and whispering. It sent a chill up my spine: These cold-eyed children were SMART's selected market, the aforementioned "gang affiliates." But so far, none of the senior membership of the Bloods (called O.G.s for "Original Gangstas") had made an appearance, which they refused to do until the place was cleared of cops. While this was being done, I felt my personal biases clouding my objectivity. Who were these kids? How did they get the power to have the police sent from a public arena? It didn't take long to find out.

> **SMART Marketing:**
>
> Once you step into the world of your target market, don't let your personal values cloud your professional judgment.

One by one, the O.G.s of the various Bounty Hunter factions began to saunter in from the rear of the gym and mingle with the crowd. As these menacing, bare-chested gang leaders maneuvered into the gym, I couldn't help but be aware that our young selected prospects (the "Baby Gs") were watching every move these guys made; they were mesmerized by their "big homies"; they hung on every word and aped every action.

The apparent leader of the group took a seat directly across from Jesse Jackson, who was flanked by Secret Service men and high-profile politicos. This leader was also flanked by his own heavy-weights. The summit began with a discussion that attributed the recent rise in gang-related homicides to the movie *Colors,* followed by accusations of the impact of gangsta rap that boomed constantly in warring neighborhoods. Accusations of programmed genocide filled the room and made the politicians and their support staff visibly uneasy. Jesse Jackson took the floor and began to make his plea for a "partnership" between the gangs and the establishment. But his speech was interrupted by a tall, wild-haired 23-year-old named Brian McLucas, better known as "Loaf." Born and bred in Nickerson Gardens, he had spent one year in Catholic school before "graduating" to the California Youth Authority. Loaf had worked his way up the Blood hierarchy. His resume included the homicide of a Grape Street Crip who had stolen his bike. Loaf was 12 at the time. By any standards, he was a hard-core career criminal. Essentially, he told Jackson and the rest of the crowd the "way it really was" in Watts, and ended with a resounding statement: "Nobody can stop this war but us!" Although I wouldn't have believed it earlier, Loaf and I had something in common after all: We knew who had to market our product, which was peace. I knew, too, that we had our point man. Now all we needed was a campaign.

THE PLAY'S THE THING

Tracy and I intercepted Loaf as he made his way out of the gym. After being introduced, I could see Loaf was initially resistant to me because of my media background; he regarded Hollywood and the music industry as part of the problem. Still he was serious about doing something to stop the war. And I made the point that if media could influence people negatively, they could motivate people positively, too. I suggested staging a play to enact the story of how the gang wars had begun. Loaf's retort was that no actor in his right mind would come to Watts to do a play. I suggested he and his homeboys be the writers and actors. This appealed to him, and we even agreed on a title: *Crossfire.*

These hard-core gang bangers were both attracted and repelled by the idea of taking their story public. Street gangs, like the Cosa

Nostra and Tong triads before them, are secret societies. Allowing themselves to become known would be making themselves targets—targets of law enforcement and targets of rival gang factions. Before Brian and his homeboys Robert Crawford (Crof Dog) and Tyrone Baker (Tystick) would allow their story to be brought to the stage, they had to consult the leadership of the Bloods, most of whom were serving triple life terms in various California penal institutions. It was agreed that we would collaborate on developing a script for the proposed stage play first. Then Loaf and Crof Dog would seek the blessings of the shot callers on death row. Within two weeks after the first draft of the script was written, we had our green light from the powers that be.

After enlisting the enthusiastic support and services of Danish film and stage director Annett Wolf, we got down to work. The campaign strategy was in place. Our medium was Brian "Loaf" McLucas and his homeboys, and the stage of the Nickerson Gardens Gym would be our delivery mechanism. Our vehicle for change was the stage play *Crossfire* written by Loaf, Crof Dog, Annett Wolf, and myself. It would chronicle Loaf's life in Nickerson Gardens and the ensuing gang warfare and would climax with an appeal for an end to the killing made by those literally in the trenches.

> **SMART Marketing:**
>
> Attract the attention of the opinion leaders in your selected market. Engage them first in your message; others will follow.

LAUNCHING THE CAMPAIGN

In the following months, I came to realize that this campaign was like countless others I had spearheaded during my 30 years in advertising—albeit the stakes were much higher. We could not effect change—that is, persuade people to buy our product—unless we gained intimate understanding of what made our audience tick. To that end, we invited the Bloods to a focus group lunch, much as we would if we were trying to determine the detergent preferences of housewives.

Taking on the role of peacemakers among the lawbreakers did, however, add a new twist to this tried-and-true marketing approach. I had to devise a way of clearly separating this stage play from the gang's criminal activities.

Finding the Right Spokesperson

Although Loaf was certainly no Michael Jordan, he was an eminently qualified and credible spokesperson to hawk our peace product to our selected market, the Baby Gs. In the past, when we wanted to attract aging baby boomers, we hired icons from their past, such as the Temptations. When we wanted to influence performance car enthusiasts for Ford Motor Company, we enlisted the California Highway Patrol, the ultimate authority figures for high-speed driving. In this situation, we knew the Baby Gs would listen to someone like Loaf.

Now all we had to do was understand why an 8-year-old would lay down his life or take the life of another in the name of gang loyalty; in short, we had to get inside the heads of members of our selected market. For this, we also depended on Loaf. As I listened to the horrific tale of life on the streets of Watts, we came to understand that street gangs are secret societies wrapped inside arcane hierarchies covered by a clandestine chain of command. They are many who move as one. Loaf said, "If we can turn our 'set' around, the rest of the sets will follow." Jackpot!

> **SMART Marketing:**
>
> Don't expect second- and thirdhand information to yield firsthand information about your audience. Make contact yourself.

Words and Music

After we transposed Loaf's painful memories to the pages of a workable—and entertaining—script, we learned how far out on a limb we had crawled. Investing select marketing approaches in a social venue can (and often does) have far graver consequences than doing so in a commercial venue. When we had a completed draft, we showed it to Tracy, who said words to the effect that "I thought it would be more . . . institutional." To which Loaf declared, "If we can't tell the truth then we ain't no better than *Colors*."

The line was drawn, with the gang reps (and SMART) on one side and the establishment reps on the other. Henceforth, we were on own own; Tracy had to withdraw support to prevent the city attorney's office from being seen as "glorifying" gang culture. The essence of selective marketing is to become one with your audience. So, although the government had started this peace initiative, we, the members of a private corporation, were being challenged to finish it.

With the true-to-life script in hand, it was up to Annett Wolf to turn our marketing mechanism into the vehicle that would sell our "product" to the select audience. Production moved to Nickerson Gardens, where 23 active and former gang members were chosen to take the bloody story of the Bounty Hunters from the streets to the stage, complete with music. During the ensuing 22 weeks of rehearsals, *Crossfire* captured the imagination and attention of the media and the public. It proved to be a wild convolution of media event and life on the streets. The *Los Angeles Times* called us a "drama gang"; television and recording stars came by, dropping words like "Broadway" and "touring company." At the same time, fistfights broke out among cast members; one of the cast was shot by a rival Crip; police instituted "gang sweeps." Through it all, rehearsals went on.

Showtime

We had accomplished what many had thought was impossible, and it was time to hit the boards. More than 3,500 people jammed Nickerson Gardens Gym. And though there was no public address system, everyone could hear every word. In fact, you could have heard the proverbial pin drop. *Crossfire* was heralded by the *Los Angeles Times* as "... the first large-scale effort by a hard-core Los Angeles street gang to redirect its antisocial energy into a positive force."

To further the effort, SMART volunteers videotaped the production, then made hundreds of copies for distribution to rival gangs. Symbolically, *Crossfire* cast member, Tystick, from the Bloods, sat down with Chopper, from the Crips, at Marie Callender's Restaurant on Wilshire Boulevard and passed the first tape. The truce process had begun.

LONG-TERM EFFECT

Sadly, since 1988, many of *Crossfire*'s cast are now dead or incarcerated, and to be sure, the gang problem is still prevalent. But did we succeed in instituting meaningful change? Ultimately, yes. The riots of 1993 vindicated our efforts, and the resultant Watts Gang Truce was publicly acknowledged to have its roots in the *Crossfire* initiatives. The truce stands today, and thousands of young lives have been spared.

And by the way, Brian "Loaf" McLucas went straight. He now heads the Crossfire Foundation, an organization that provides free computer instruction and access to the Internet for Nickerson Gardens youth. His work was recently featured on the front page of the *Wall Street Journal*.

Select Marketing Lessons

Without question, "social marketing" teaches unique lessons. First, at SMART, we learned that by taking on a controversial cause, we became controversial by association. During our Watts peace marketing campaign, many of SMART's other clients became "uncomfortable" with our activities. While we were busy trying to reflect the values of one client (the gangs), other clients felt their values were being misrepresented.

Second, while it is always imperative to gather firsthand information from a target audience, this is particularly important when promoting a public-service campaign. It's also essential to have access to political intelligence and "plugged-in" advisors. Not to do this guarantees failure.

Third, when working on public causes, personal passion can cloud objectivity and cause professionals to lose perspective. Communications pros must resist the "white knight" syndrome and remember that their job is to produce the product that makes change possible; they can't ever change people's values. They can only be influenced to initiate change.

6

CHICKEN FIGHT:

Carving a Niche in a Crowded Coop

for Hardee's Restaurants

- **Market:** Sports fans of all ages.

- **Marketing Challenge:** Distinguish Hardee's as an alternative to both fast food and sit-down restaurants by adding chicken to its menu.

- **Marketing Solution:** Use an admirable sports figure to introduce Hardee's fried chicken. At the time, no quick-service restaurant sold both hamburgers and chicken.

- **Outcome:** Chicken became the most successful new product launch in Hardee's history.

What's a food chain to do when it's not fast enough to be fast food like McDonald's or Burger King, but not formal enough to be a sit-down restaurant like Denny's, the corner diner, or the local pub? That's the limbo in which Hardee's found itself in 1993. The fast-food "value meal wars" had just begun, and Hardee's, with its $3.89 cheeseburgers, could not hope to compete with the 99¢ Whopper. Nor did it have a chance in the already troubled sit-down restaurant category. Hardee's had to rethink its entire business strategy before it could hope to carve out a niche in the quick-service restaurant (QSR) category. At the time, Hardee's Food Systems enjoyed sales of $3.93 billion, with 3,963 restaurants nationwide; it was the fourth largest chain in the QSR category, but it wanted to do better.

Hardee's concluded that if it couldn't compete on price, it would compete on completeness of menu, and the restaurant decided to add fried chicken to its bill of fare. To gain access to that segment of the market, Hardee's acquired the Roy Rogers chicken chain; sales jumped to $4 billion and the number of outlets grew to 3,997. The Roy Rogers fried chicken recipe had proven successful in the Northeast, so the Hardee's marketing objective was to induce trial among its current and prospective customers in the North- and Southeast, the Midwest, and the Rocky Mountain states. The main competition in this market was Kentucky Fried Chicken (KFC)— tough competition indeed. The fried chicken arena is a retail-oriented, price-point-driven product category whose customers are fiercely brand loyal, and where price promotion dominates the marketing mix of the top-seated brands. Gaining market share for a new entrant is a difficult task.

PLAYING CHICKEN

Hardee's selected as its urban markets ad agency Glover & Potter in Chicago which worked with SMART in Los Angeles to develop a strategy to introduce chicken to current and prospective Hardee's customers in 22 television markets. Through consumer focus groups and qualitative research, we determined that this could not be successfully accomplished through price-point promotional efforts alone. Hardee's had to be repositioned as a credible pur-veyor of fried chicken to reduce resistance to trial. For a cost-conscious outfit like Hardee's Food Systems, outspending the competition was not an option. We had to outmarket them. And since the rollout was considered a test, we had to make it happen faster, cheaper, and better than the ongoing national effort.

As much as 75 percent of new product introductions fail in test markets. There are many ways in which market segmentation can improve those odds. Certainly, developmental research conducted on a segment-by-segment basis is the first step in determining the needs and desires of the marketplace. We learned that the "what and where to eat" questions resulted in dissension among most families. The addition of chicken to the Hardee's menu intended to solve that problem by creating a one-stop eatery.

Test Anxiety

The decision was made to conduct taste tests comparing the new Hardee's chicken, category leader KFC's Original Recipe, and Church's. Hardee's won by an overwhelming majority. With that information in hand, Hardee's general market agency, Ogilvy & Mather, made the first move with hard-hitting, retail-oriented consumer testimonials.

Like many cost-conscious marketers, Hardee's engaged an overall general market ad agency for mass-marketing efforts but hedged its bets by bringing in specialists in ethnic marketing to African Americans or Hispanics as warranted by their products' usage in those markets. The truth of the matter is that these specialized agencies generally can do more with less than their general-market colleagues—especially in the areas of media cost per thousand and TV commercial production expenditures. SMART was brought in by Glover & Potter because of our demonstrated abilities to develop segment-specific creative and carry through with cost-efficient production techniques.

Although store traffic increased initially, it soon began to trail off. Clearly, we needed a more effective offensive weapon.

SPECIAL DELIVERY

It came serendipitously in the form of NBA all-star Karl "The Mailman" Malone, the Utah Jazz's power forward superstar. He had approached Terratron, a Hardee's franchise group operator and offered to do some local promotional advertising, and in exchange Hardee's would use his trucking company to transport its produce interstate.

> **SMART Marketing:**
>
> Be open to opportunities that fall into your lap at the local level. They may have national implications later on.

Malone's reputation was unassailable; his persona is that of a no-nonsense, honest, hardworking "good guy," whose movie-star looks and charisma appeal to both men and women. Glover & Potter and SMART convinced Hardee's that Malone could deliver for the chain the way he delivered on court.

Our creative strategy called for Malone to slam-dunk Hardee's on KFC's home court, Salt Lake City, where Colonel Sanders had opened his first Kentucky Fried Chicken outlet. Salt Lake City also happens to be home to the Utah Jazz and the base for their devoted legion of fans—who became our selected market.

> **SMART Marketing:**
>
> When using a celebrity endorser, find out how that celebrity is perceived by the target customers before creating a role for him or her to play. If the customers don't believe the seller, they won't buy the product.

Our first commercial featured Malone giving his pitch directly to the camera: "I told Hardee's if their chicken didn't taste as good as KFC's, I wasn't gonna say it did." The Mailman played like a solid-gold hero in the conservative western, midwestern, and southern states that were the initial test bed for Hardee's fried chicken. Overnight, our client became a player in the chicken category.

TAKING IT TO THE NET

At first, using a celebrity endorser in the local market was looked upon as an interesting addendum to the test campaign. But it quickly became apparent just how powerful a select market and a select market strategy can be to the success of a product when they are perfectly matched. The force of Karl Malone and the passion of basketball fans was a select marketer's dream come true.

Because Hardee's had more or less backed into the relationship with Malone at the regional level, the national brand group under the direction of Jim Gregory and Hardee's marketing head Gerry Gramaglia were more concerned with giving legs to their competitive strategy than developing one around a celebrity spokesperson. It was Gregory, an avid hoops fan, who recognized the potential a relationship with the Mailman might afford the brand.

In addition to being an NBA icon (he was named one of the NBA's top 50 players of all time), Malone was not overexposed in product endorsements, making his alignment with Hardee's all the more believable. Hardee's Food Systems is a strange duck among QSR chain outlets. Although its restaurants stretch from Baltimore to Salt Lake City, Hardee's purposefully has stayed out of major markets like New York and Los Angeles because of the high media and operations costs. As a result, the company is a heavy spot or local television user but hardly ever buys network TV time. This unique arrangement allows Hardee's to test market products locally and then roll them out, spot TV market by spot TV market, until they are virtually national in scope.

The result of the nationwide spot television campaign featuring Karl "The Mailman" Malone? The Hardee's fried chicken market exploded. Within six months, sales in some areas increased as much as 25 percent. In addition to the television commercials, Malone was featured on billboards and promotional giveaways. A special Mailman takeout chicken box was designed in the shape of his famous big rig that he drives during the off-season, and suddenly Hardee's chicken was causing store traffic jams.

Fanning the Flames

Even though the Utah Jazz has never won an NBA championship, Karl Malone is regarded as one of the consummate winners in the game. His commitment to the game and the team (he is one of a very few players to have stayed with the same team for his entire career) made him the ideal product spokesperson. These qualities made him believable to this targeted market—sports fans. Believability is key to the success of any marketing campaign. More important, it points out the necessity and value of understanding the selected market, which then makes it possible to determine how or through whom to reach that market.

Select Marketing Lessons

As pioneers in selective marketing techniques, we at SMART learned early that the *culture* of a particular market segment has a greater impact on what its members do than any other influence. In this case study, the culture of sports fans is consistent with that of any other enthusiast group. They define themselves by their special interest and by the stars in that galaxy—here, a sports hero.

Marketers, especially selective marketers, would be wise never to underestimate the power of these attachments. Celebrity endorsements are not new, but they are more prevalent then ever, and they pose special and very high risks (as the Hertz–O. J. relationship has proven). The successful campaign must be a delicately formed triumvirate of product, market, and spokesperson.

7

MODERN STONE AGE MARKETING:

Reaching Several Corporate Select Markets

for Turner Home Entertainment

- **Market:** Corporate marketing, merchandising, and brand management decision makers.

- **Marketing Challenge:** Convince traditional brand management decision makers of the wisdom of adding value to their products through the licensing of Hanna-Barbera animated characters.

- **Marketing Solution:** Establish a preference for Turner's recently acquired Hanna-Barbera properties by using a variety of trade periodicals to build awareness and acceptance.

- **Outcome:** Turner Licensing & Merchandising developed more than 500 domestic and international licensees, including Mattel Toys, Kraft Foods, Lewis Galoob Toys, Arby's, and Days Inn. With products in more than 40 product categories and offices in New York, London, and Hong Kong, Turner received the licensing industry's top award for 1994's best international program for *The Flintstones*.

I n 1997, retail sales of licensed merchandise in the United States and Canada topped $73 billion. This indicates that prospects will buy from a name they trust even if that name has nothing to do with the maker of the product. If you manufacture or distribute a nonbranded item, licensing the image of a well-known character can give your product the instant recognition and credibility of an internationally known brand at a fraction of the cost. It's like renting a brand name. This and this alone *adds value* to your nonbranded garment, lunch box, vitamin, or breakfast cereal, making it equal, if not superior, to your branded competitor. Quick—name *three* major players in the children's vitamin category that *do not* reside in Bedrock.

> **SMART Marketing:**
>
> What makes a population segment into a market segment is the identification and understanding of that particular group's values, needs, and desires and the skillful application of those elements to make the sale.

By setting *The Flintstones* in the Stone Age and making the rest of the characters' values, needs, and desires consistent with America's most lucrative market segment (suburban America), Joseph Hanna and William Barbera ensured their success for decades after their network TV run became history. *Universal appeal* is what makes the Flintstones, the Jetsons, and all of their wacky buddies perennial favorites. And that appeal is what makes them highly valuable licensing properties to boomers and their offspring. Of course, Fred and Wilma had a long way to go to catch up to licensing giants like Mickey and Bugs.

FRED AND WILMA GET SMART

In 1994, SMART was brought in by Turner Licensing & Merchandising (Ted Turner having recently bought Hanna-Barbera Studios) to sell that line of logic to decision makers in the marketing, promotion, and merchandising departments of corporate America.

With Steven Spielberg set to produce *The Flintstones* movie and John Goodman signed to play Fred, there was absolutely no question that this modern Stone Age family was about to enjoy a rebirth in popularity in 1994. But all was not as rosy as it might seem. Now there would be two Freds in the marketplace—the Fred Flintstone we all knew, loved, and grew up with and Roseanne's TV husband. SMART's assignment was to sell the selected markets—packaged goods, fashion, toy makers, and gift and stationery manufacturers—on the merits of the original Hanna-Barbera version. The John Goodman version was Universal Studios' and Amblin' Entertainment's opportunity to shine.

> **SMART Marketing:**
>
> Shared values are one of the most compelling reasons for a selected market's entertainment choices and preferences.

How Did We Yabba-Dabba-Do It?

Quantitative research may distort reality, while qualitative research may bring enlightenment. In other words, a nationwide phone poll to 1,500 moviegoers about their interest in seeing John Goodman as Fred Flintstone may predict success at the box office. The research supplied by a roomful of ten baby boomer guys being given a choice between the cartoon Fred and the live-action Fred on a T-shirt may prevent disaster at the point of sale. We found out that real fat guys (most of us boomers have a weight problem) don't like wearing pictures of other real fat guys on their bellies. This told us that our Fred (the Hanna-Barbera version) was destined to be the big winner in *The Flintstones* movie blitz that was sure to come. Early information is worth its weight in dinosaur eggs.

> **SMART Marketing:**
>
> Licensed products are specifically developed to the interests the licenser perceives to be representative of their properties' audience. As the audience expands, the range of products broadens.

The difference between opinion and experience can mean the difference between success and failure. Turner Licensing & Merchandising Vice President, Nancy McCreedy, and Director of Marketing, David Palmer, wanted to hit the ground running with a full-blown advertising blitz in the marketing and media trades. By targeting key influencers first, we could presell their clients. Our launch strategy was to let the heat from the Spielberg Flintstones create a "window of awareness" for the original Flintstones and pull-through for the Jetsons, Tom & Jerry, Yogi Bear, Johnny Quest, and Scooby-Doo.

We Have Met the Target and They Are Us

Lack of understanding can be very dangerous indeed when your advertising is directed to opinion leaders who can influence the allocation of millions. Such is the challenge of business-to-business marketing. Luckily for us, our client was a seasoned marketing practitioner who had made her bones on Madison Avenue at Ogilvy & Mather. Nancy McCreedy knew exactly who our first target was: herself.

Our position was that our selected market would be as thrilled about working with the Flintstones as we were—so thrilled that they would communicate their excitement to their clients, the brand management decision makers. So we launched our first ads in *Adweek, Media Week,* and *Advertising Age.*

Our big idea was to let the characters be themselves. SMART decided early on never to let them slip out of character and become merely cute and memorable designs or gimmicks. We set out to use the ad page as Hanna-Barbera would. More important, we knew we had to focus hard on selective marketing's primary objective: profiling our target market carefully and completely. SMART's initial task was to identify and determine how to reach this elite, fast-moving, and hard-to-hit market. Identifying these people was the easy part. Here are the demographics we determined for mass merchandising and marketing decision makers and their key influencers:

- They number approximately 7,500 individuals nationwide.
- They are generally high-energy, 40-something go-getters living in a world of market share points and media costs per thousand.
- They work on the move, attending meetings and traveling in the field, making dozens of decisions an hour and affecting the standard of living in many third-world nations.
- They think and speak of "footprints," the number of square inches of floor space a given point-of-purchase display will require, and how much revenue the given item must earn in the footprint to meet their quarterly sales projections.
- They belong to one or more industry organizations and seek their decision-making information from their colleagues as well as their competitors.
- They track vigilantly the information published in their respective trade publications such as *Discount Store News, Gift & Stationery Business, Brand Week, Advertising Age, Index, Giftware News, Playthings, Earnshaw's, Toy Show,* and dozens of newsletters.
- They are continuously bombarded with new product deals, ideas, and pitches and therefore are not so easy to impress.

SMARTER THAN THE AVERAGE BEAR

What came out of the deep attitude and values inquiries and deliberations at SMART was a clearer understanding of how certain corporate decision makers make emotional decisions, then justify them intellectually, and others make intellectual decisions based upon the emotions of others.

In many cases it came down to "I love Fred Flintstone" or "My boss loves Fred Flintstone; let's see what Fred can do to help me move my clawhammers." So we decided to sell the relationship. We urged these decision makers to "put Fred or George or Yogi on your team," to "use Astro on your doggy product," to imagine "you and Fred against St. Joseph's aspirin for children." How can you lose if you "'Toon Up Your Brand," as the ads in *Brand Week, Ad Age,* and *Media Decisions* urged, with Fred, George Jetson, Tom & Jerry, and the whole crew perched rebus-style in the typographically elegant oversized text.

> **SMART Marketing:**
>
> The toy market spent $20 billion in 1995. Nearly half of those sales were on licensed merchandise—each with its own built-in selected market.

SMART believed early on that the classic animated character line would outperform dolls that looked like John Goodman and Rick Moranis instead of Fred and Barney. They were already loaded and ready to move. As things turned out, we were right by a lot.

'TOON IN TO YOUR MARKET

Exactly how does SMART determine the effective demand potential of a given population segment? What techniques work best? Well, in addition to trolling cyberspace for the factual data that gives bone structure to our "selected relationship models," our account planners also institute "on-site listening probes" in locations where the agency can identify specific functions or events that are of interest to our selected audience. Airports, professional seminars, golf clinics, trade shows—these are just a few of the locations we visited to find out how our funny friends would play to corporate decision makers. Wherever more than three of our client's selected market decision makers were known to congregate and converse, we were listening. Eavesdropping is the heart and soul of determining the wants, needs, and desires of our subject.

The experiential data and observations gleaned from these listening probes gave context to the factual data gathered by more traditional methodologies. These observations supply the vital organs to the selected relationship model we use at SMART to dimensionalize our selected customers and the world they live in, work for, and react to.

Key to each of our selective marketing campaigns for Turner Home Entertainment was the determination of each market segment's infrastructure. Understanding the decision-making process as it happened across several lines of business would be the factor most critical to our success.

> **SMART Marketing:**
>
> Identify, then profile in detail, who your target market is, how you can find out the way they think and operate, and where they can be reached. Without this information, no project can get off the ground.

To acquire this knowledge, we first identified and ranked by sales volume the top ten product categories in the licensing and merchandising arena. After identifying those ten categories, SMART surveyed each category for the most respected trade vehicle. This was accomplished by telephone-polling secretaries and assistants about their bosses' trade magazine subscriptions. The type of digging SMART undertakes shows rather graphically that the work of mining a market segment is inescapably the work of acquiring local rather than universal knowledge.

YOU NEVER HEARD OF 2 STUPID DOGS? ASK YOUR KIDS

The most enlightened element of Turner Home Entertainment's promotion of the well-known Hanna-Barbera family of funny friends to corporate America was inviting their lesser-known cousins along for the ride. Hoping for classic status by association, our campaign presented a litany of Hanna-Barbera star-toons with such characters as Captain Planet, Swat Kats, and my personal favorite, 2 Stupid Dogs. Though each were lesser-known players in the jungle that is Saturday morning television, the strategy was a sound one in that it added the value of the Hanna-Barbera "brand" to the newer characters' corporate profiles as well as giving smaller companies with more limited budgets an entrée into the lucrative licensing and merchandising arena.

> **SMART Marketing:**
>
> Find out who has the money (or market) for your product, then focus your efforts on selling it to them.

Right off the bat we determined the profit potential of each of the given business segments—accessories, advertising tie-ins (ad agencies), apparel, confection, entertainment, food and beverage, gifts and novelties, health and beauty aids, housewares, package goods, publishing, textiles, and toys and games. We went to animation dealers to spot trends. These methods of strategic conversation made with representative members of our selected audiences gave us critical insights into exactly how the need for peer or social approval might influence their decision to buy. And when all else failed, we asked our kids.

What If Hertz Had Hired Mr. Jetson instead of Mr. Simpson?

By understanding the purchase process of each of our selected markets, we become better equipped to help influence the outcome in our client's favor. Intelligence gathering at SMART goes "way deep."

The one thing we learned that was constant through all of our background research was that many of the marketing decisions being reached by our selected audience were made as a result of fear. They generally chose the alternative that posed the least amount of risk.

This information, coupled with the growing number of reports linking sports and entertainment luminaries with criminal behavior and unsavory lifestyles, yielded our core strategy. George Jetson was unlikely to be busted on a morals charge anytime within what's left of this century. Cartoon endorsers are infinitely more risk-free than celebrity endorsers. And so our core strategy was born.

> CREATIVE STRATEGY: Convince corporate America that a marketing partnership with a Hanna-Barbera cartoon character brings with it all the years of goodwill you've grown up with and none of the risks associated with celebrity tie-ins.

At last we had a premise that could convince marketing executives that a relationship with Fred Flintstone or any one of his pals was worth giving up their closely guarded, risk-adverse promotional dollars for. So we ran with it—and it worked.

In 1996, Turner Licensing & Merchandising was folded into the Consumer Products division of Warner Bros. as a result of the acquisition of Turner by Time Warner. Now Fred and Bugs are members of the same cartoon family.

Select Marketing Lessons

The following lessons can be drawn from our experience in reaching corporate decision makers:

1. Corporate prospects buy from names that they trust and that they believe their consumers will trust.

2. Bonds of trust that have been established through people's life experiences can sometimes be utilized to influence them in their roles as corporate decision makers.

3. Sensitivity to business sensibilities and values in the development of a segmented marketing strategy geared toward corporate decision makers is critical.

4. Immersing yourself in the "cultural ecosystem" of the corporate decision maker's industry *before* initiating your selective marketing program is key to its success.

5. Determining the effectiveness of the corporate decision maker's impact upon the sale *before* setting up your selective marketing program allows you to determine who *all* the players are and to include them in your sales effort.

6. The effect of cultural, professional, or geographic behavior patterns on the corporate decision maker's awareness and retention of your sales message should be factored into your selective marketing program. The fewer the number of decision makers, the more tailored the possibilities for each sales message become.

7. The market potential for a product or service targeted to corporate decision makers can be deter-

mined only by exposure to the prospects themselves. Qualitative research is the key.

8. To determine the needs potential for your product or service to corporate decision makers, consult with trade journalists and securities analysts in the fields run by your selected prospects. Just remember, these are not secure channels of communication.

9. To determine the effective demand potential of your product or service, offer it on a limited-time, deeply discounted basis to a corporate decision maker. If the answer is no, the demand potential will probably be low at the standard price among industry followers who make up the bulk of most markets.

10. It is practically impossible to determine the profit potential of a "yes" from a corporate decision maker—especially if it results in a significant increase in sales for the decision maker's company.

8

YOUR PLACE OR MINE?

Advertising to the Advertisers

for the BelAge Hotel

- **Market:** Business travelers to Los Angeles, California.

- **Marketing Challenge:** The nine properties of L'Ermitage Hotels chain were losing business to each other.

- **Marketing Solution:** Develop industry-specific sales campaigns for each of the nine L'Ermitage properties in the West Hollywood/Beverly Hills market.

- **Outcome:** All the properties became successful in their respective markets.

L'Ermitage Hotels chain owned and operated eight luxury all-suite hotels in the West Hollywood/Beverly Hills area and one in Santa Barbara. Most had been opened in anticipation of capturing the influx of travelers coming to enjoy the 1984 Summer Olympics in Los Angeles. Subsequently, however, because of widespread area violence, threats of terrorism, and fear of earthquakes, the hordes of anticipated Olympics visitors did not show up. The windfall profits anticipated by the hotel chain did not materialize during the games or following them. L.A. was also experiencing an epidemic of runaway television and movie production that also heavily impacted the occupancy levels of the west-side hotels. And it was not enough that circumstances—indeed, Mother Nature herself—seemed to be conspiring against the business, but the nine sibling hotels began competing with one another to stay afloat.

Something had to be done, and done fast, to forestall further massive shortfalls to projected revenues. SMART was brought in to bring order to chaos, and L'Ermitage would prove to be a significant test of the selective marketing principles that SMART promulgated.

TO EACH ITS OWN

It was quickly determined that the best way to stop the internal feeding frenzy off of one market segment was to refocus each of the nine hotels to a single, very specific, very *selective* market segment. This would put an immediate stop to the duplication of effort that had plagued the hotel chain following the close of the Olympic games.

Here's how we reassigned the audiences for the hotels:

- For the Mondrian, we targeted the rock music industry.

- Le Park got R & B, dance, Latin, and rap artists.

- Le Rêve and Le Dufy shared the fashion and interior design trades, because of their proximity to the L.A. Design Center.

- The namesake hotel, L'Ermitage, was given Century City's "legal eagles" and off-shore finance travelers who preferred a Beverly Hills address.

- BelAge was positioned as the perfect hotel for commercial-producing advertising professionals and their Fortune 500 clients.

- Valadon was targeted to the budget-conscious Beverly Hills visitors who were traveling for recreation rather than business.

- Cézanne was positioned as a long-term residence for music and motion picture technical professionals and executives.

- Petite L'Ermitage, adjacent to the flagship hotel, was marketed as the perfect place for recuperating from the effects of surgical or other invasive medical procedures.

- El Escoreal, the Santa Barbara property, was promoted to the guests of the other eight hotels as the perfect weekend getaway from whatever business had brought them to Los Angeles in the first place.

Although SMART developed advertising for all the hotels, to explain how we worked this multilayered selective marketing strategy, this chapter describes one of those campaigns: The advertising SMART targeted to the advertising industry for the BelAge Hotel. Of the selected markets just described, the commercial production people promised to be the most difficult to reach. They were, after all, in "the business" and presumably immune to—or at least inoculated against—the seductions of the well-turned phrase and compelling imagery. Furthermore, most members of the target audience were practitioners of mass-marketing programs, so it would be a tough proving ground for selective marketing techniques and principles.

WHO'S BEEN SLEEPING IN MY BED?

As always, and as I repeat elsewhere in this book, the first step was to identify, define, and describe, in as much detail as possible, our target customers, and then, more specifically, to determine which of their needs were and were not being met by the hotels they frequented.

With hundreds of commercials under my belt, my first inclination was to "focus-group" myself. When a marketer him- or herself is a member of a target audience, self-examination is not a bad—and often can be a good—place to begin. But as I admonish elsewhere, this should never be considered enough.

To proceed with the research into the target audience for BelAge, we derived, from the broader guest-list database, a list of commercial agency guests who currently stayed at the hotel. To generate a focus group, I sent complimentary breakfast invitations for twenty of those guests. Nine responded, and our research began.

Cleaning Up the Mess

Those nine complimentary breakfasts taught me just how much I didn't know about others in my profession, especially regarding their needs—and, more important, their unmet needs—when on business trips. It also didn't take long to discern that our client, the BelAge, was dropping the ball, and all because of what we came to refer to as "Le Shit," the phoniness often inherent in European-inspired restaurants, hotels, and nightspots, which seemed to be the justification for rude, officious, and offensive behavior and/or indifferent levels of service by employees of such establishments. Our research had revealed that members of the target market—advertising professionals—were turned off by the snotty attitude of the staff and patronized the hotel only because of the space proffered by the multiroom suite accommodations, which functioned as offices-away-from-the-office. Furthermore, our target patrons were becoming increasingly disgruntled by slow phone response

times and message unreliability. It didn't take a member of the
Hilton family to realize that this was a market ripe for the picking
by any competitor wise enough to address the unmet needs of the
BelAge's guests.

Clearly, our first job was to convince the client that an attitude
adjustment was in order on the part of its staff. From those early
morning breakfasts, I had relearned the importance of cultivating
both sympathy and empathy for the needs of the selected customer.
Now I had to make the client see that this was the perspective from
which to begin to determine the ways the current service was failing to meet those needs. This was easier said than done, because
many department managers and staff members believed that the
current attitude was essential to the ambience of the hotel and jus-
tified the premium-priced room rates and service fee structure.
"Holiday Inns are warm and fuzzy. We are the BelAge" was the
response we initially received when voicing our concerns about
customers' feelings toward the hotel.

As with many clients who find themselves under siege by plum-
meting sales and escalating operating costs, the only way we could
convince L'Ermitage Hotels to dump "Le Shit" for a policy of customer service über alles was to bring to the company's attention
the tactics being used by the competition to erode its market share.
First we did daily tallies of the occupancy rates of the competing
hotels. Staff members of the competitors were persuaded to provide us with information and weekly examples of how long-term
customers were being enticed away. For instance, the staff was "too
busy" at L'Ermitage to press a guest's pair of slacks for a pending
dinner engagement. Somehow this information was transmitted to
the Four Seasons three blocks away and the L'Ermitage guest was
spirited away by the manager of the Four Seasons with an offer of
a complimentary dinner, a lower room rate for a larger suite, a lim-
ousine to effect the transfer of accommodations, and, of course,

those slacks pressed and delivered to the customer's suite 30 minutes after checking into the Four Seasons. After several such reports of above-and-beyond responses by their watchful competitors to the unmet wants, needs, and desires of their patrons, the management of the L'Ermitage began to see the wisdom of jettisoning their "Le Shit" pretenses for a more proactive stance regarding customer satisfaction and retention.

Once we had hoteliers extraordinaire Severyn and Arnold Ashkenazy on our side, they graciously acceded to our recommendations to implement new systems and attitudes in the housekeeping and guest service staffs. The Ashkenazy brothers had built their hotel empire by converting their family-owned apartment buildings into luxury all-suite hotels. They were the pioneers of the trend toward all-suite hotels geared to the business traveler, and our findings spurred these innovators into immediate action.

> **SMART Marketing:**
>
> Don't be so sure you know the reasons your customers are your customers. Ask them. What you learn may surprise you.

YOUR BUSINESS IS MY BUSINESS

> **SMART Marketing:**
>
> Identify every point within an organization that has contact with the target market. Designate those areas as potential points of sale, and make sure staff are trained to respond accordingly.

Le Shit was banished forever, and the importance of being an extension of the guests' business activities became paramount. The BelAge staff was instructed that the hotel was repositioning itself as *the* hotel in the area for the television commercial industry's agency and client organizations. They were told to consider themselves a part of that industry. Henceforth, every message, call, or package directed to members of that profession was to be regarded as time-critical. They were also alerted to the fact that new hotels being built in the area would be competitors for the BelAge's guests.

SUITE OF DREAMS

Speaking frankly and honestly to service providers and listening closely and openly to service recipients were the first steps in preparing BelAge for its more competitive environment. Our segment study of the commercial professional market had identified more than 100 service improvements that BelAge could make to tailor itself to the ad executive in town to produce commercials. To be sure, some of the improvements were purely illusionary. For example, Mondrian Competitor, the Sunset Marquis, displayed gold records won by guests Cyndi Lauper and Mick Jagger on the walls of the hotel bar. Those gold records did more to position the Sunset Marquis to music industry pros than any mere ad in *Billboard* could ever convey. But illusion is one of the hallmarks of an excellent selective marketing campaign. Clive Davis, head of Arista Records, recently lamented that "everybody is having a lifestyle marketed to them." That is what happens when the wires show. To be truly successful, selective marketing must be engaging, never offensive; a guest, never an intruder.

> **SMART Marketing:**
>
> "He whose bread I eat, that's the song I sing." If you target a specific business, then that's the business you're in.

Call Me
Our goal for the BelAge was that it be elevated to first-called status among ad people traveling from Chicago, Minneapolis, Detroit, St. Louis, Dallas, Houston, Pittsburgh, Atlanta, Washington, Philadelphia, Boston, and New York City. To accomplish this,

we first focused on impressing the advertising professionals who were already patrons of the BelAge.

Once we had identified who it was we were out to impress, the BelAge staff and management shifted into high gear. They knew that our selective marketing efforts would be only as effective as the knowledge their employees had of the target market. To ensure that staff always had updated information, check-in data indicated the industry of the guest, agency communities were assiduously tracked, room questionnaires were continually tabulated, and the hotel's services continued to be more finely tuned to the guests' needs. A new phone system was installed and the occupancy rate began to rise.

Pennywise

Complicating the campaign strategy, however, was that it had to be very cost-effective. The crushing weight of overdevelopment had taken its toll on the Ashkenazy empire of small, all-suite luxury hotels. And protracted disputes with the city and neighbors were also debilitating the company. SMART worked with L'Ermitage's director of creative services, Monica Erne, and barter agents MRI to build a $2-million war chest through bartered media time paid for in hotel room nights.

We also worked to generate a buzz in the ad communities in our target cities. This was accomplished by developing for each of the hotels industry-specific newsletters that would be sent to former guests on a quarterly basis. These newsletters would tell ad industry recipients which ad campaigns were being produced by noted hotel guests, what star directors were booking their productions into the hotel, what Oscar parties were being held in hotel ballrooms, and what recording artists were in town to cut their latest chart-topping albums. The appearance of entertainment notables at BelAge went a long way toward attracting the ad professionals we were targeting.

Star Light, Star Bright

And because it would have been foolish in Los Angeles to discount star power, the Ashkenazys wisely extended themselves to the movie industry. They offered hotel suites to movie studios to use for interview purposes; to Hollywood's favorite charities, they made banquet facilities available. In this way, real cachet was established, and visiting ad people were made to feel like Hollywood insiders. This approach differed from the old "Le Shit" of faux-European snobbery, which our target market had found offensive, because the new image capitalized on Hollywood's movie star snobbery—which Madison Avenue sponsors and therefore believes itself to be part and parcel of.

PRINT IT!

Once we were well on the path to service readiness, we began to craft the message. We knew that to use imprecise terms in our advertising would be to dampen the effectiveness of our selective marketing initiative. We had to launch BelAge into the production process and then establish its importance as a vital link in navigating that process successfully. With the hotel set to back up our advertising promotions, SMART created a highly targeted print campaign that positioned the BelAge as the place to "come home to" after long, tiring days in the commercial production trenches. Our full-page ads ran in the trades: *Brand Week, Adweek, Backstage, Shoots,* and *Variety.* We hit our target audience twice a month for two years, using 14 different scenarios to which all ad production professionals could relate.

The careful work we had done beforehand at the hotel level backed up our campaign promises. Our second objective was met, and occupancy rates began to climb.

Footnote: Unfortunately, L'Ermitage's financial problems could not be resolved and Interstate Hotels, the funding bank's management company took control of the chain. However, the value of selective marketing was not lost on the new owners, and they continued with our program. The BelAge went on to become an institution in the advertising community.

Select Marketing Lessons

In today's complex markets, scale no longer ensures significant cost advantages. More often, it is selective marketing that provides those advantages. Far more easily than mass-marketing practices, selective marketing principles make it possible to achieve a true level of understanding between you and the customer you are trying to reach, just by virtue of the fact that it is a smaller audience. That in turn enables you to reach them more effectively. A market segment is any group of people who could sit down with each other and have enough in common to carry on a reasonably meaningful conversation. Try having a meaningful conversation in a room full of people, each of whom has different interests, values, and belief systems. That's what mass marketing requires and why it so often fails. When you can market essentially one on one, obviously the results can be more meaningful to the customer.

The BelAge case study teaches that selective marketing can be used even on an intracompany basis, that multidivisional or chain companies trying to feed off of one market segment may do so at their peril. By finding the segments within a given market, selective marketing can open the door to new markets and greater possibilities for reaching them.

9

MARKETING THE MISUNDERSTOOD:

Linking Product Identity with Consumer Identity

for Dr Pepper

- **Market:** Young, hip, urban adults; the counter-culture.

- **Marketing Challenge:** Expand the regional, rural market for a soft drink into urban centers.

- **Marketing Solution:** Tap into the feelings of disenfranchisement of the selected market, and use alternative media for that purpose.

- **Outcome:** Dr Pepper became the third most popular soft drink in America.

It was 1972. Baby boomers were still being regarded by the mainstream as the "counterculture." But merchandisers had started to recognize that counter though they may be, what this large audience thought about and considered important counted a lot toward the success or failure of many products and services. So when the soft drink company Dr Pepper, whose primary customer base was southern and rural, wanted to expand its reach in the Northeast and Midwest, it decided to go after the young, urban, hip, bored-with-cola crowd—which was then also being aggressively courted by 7UP, the Uncola.

Dr Pepper, an independent company, knew what it was up against, so to get a foot in the door, its management convinced Coca-Cola Bottlers in New York, Chicago, and Los Angeles to bottle and distribute its soft drink. In return for their considerable clout, the Coke bottlers required that Dr Pepper support its expansion with a considerable advertising budget. To avoid conflicts of interest, McCann-Erickson, Coca-Cola's advertising agency, recommended that Dr Pepper use Young & Rubicam, where I was then working. This was a logical choice since Y&R had a jump start in the forms of Burt Blum, an agency art director who was also freelancing for a Coke-owned Dr Pepper taste-alike called Mr. Pibb; Jim Millman, another Y&R art director; and copywriters Irv Weinberg and Brian Olesky, who had freelanced a spectacular Dr Pepper campaign for the Burt Wells Agency before Y&R got the assignment. Our team worked under the direction of associate creative director Mike Sclosberg. In addition, Y&R was given creative free reign. Furthermore, we knew that advertising had to talk to its market, not its makers. We were pioneers in the field of segmented, or selective, marketing, thanks in great part to our work on Eastern Airlines and General Foods accounts.

DEFINING THE INDEFINABLE

There was just one problem: Young & Rubicam had never handled a soft drink account. We had no experience or knowledge of the category. That had to change in a hurry. Then there was the matter of money; mediawise, there would not be a lot of it—no network prime time to clear up America's misconceptions about this soft drink from the sticks.

But what the creative team at Y&R didn't know about the traits and habits of the typical Dr Pepper consumer, they certainly knew how to find out. In selective marketing, one of the first objectives of any program is to become a part of the targeted consumer's way of life. Working at the edge of a trendsetting market segment requires keeping up with your customers' ever changing wants and needs. We conducted one of the most extensive research studies of the soft drink industry ever launched. It didn't take long to recognize that we had our work cut out for us. We learned that:

> **SMART Marketing:**
>
> Whereas mass marketing must deal in lowest-common-denominator terms to ensure an all-inclusive reach, because selective marketing aims only at a selected prospect, it can fine-tune a campaign.

- Most people who were polled could not describe what Dr Pepper tasted like; it was variously compared to everything from medicine to prune juice to pepper sauce. Nothing else tasted like Dr Pepper and Dr Pepper tasted like nothing else.

- Many respondents said their only knowledge of the brand came from the wintertime "Drink It HOT" Dr Pepper commercials done by Dick Clark on *American Bandstand* in the early 1960s.

- No one surveyed understood the significance of the 10, 2, and 4 on the Dr Pepper label.

- No one had a clue what the drink was made of.

Like many brands that make the leap from regional to national distribution, the data gathered from people who did not use the product in the expansion markets became even more important than the data gathered from the brand's current users on the brand's home turf. A great number of those polled could only remember Dr Pepper from their days of military service on bases in the South. No product (other than automobiles) so defines those who use it as soft drinks. The image of down-home rednecks swigging Dr Pepper is quite the opposite of the image of effete Northeasterners sipping their Pepsi Generation refreshment or Midwestern iconoclasts enjoying their "Uncola," 7UP. Coca-Cola chairman and CEO, Roberto C. Goizueta, said it best when he stated, "Coca-Cola's primary product is not soft drinks. It is soft drink advertising."

In with the In Crowd

Downstairs in the creative department, as I and my colleagues pondered what to do with all this research that told us nobody knew anything about this brand we were charged with promoting, somebody cradled a bottle of Dr Pepper and jokingly said, "Aww, poor baby; so misunderstood." From his lips to the lips of a million consumers! We had our tag line:

Dr Pepper: America's Most Misunderstood Soft Drink

From there, it was just a matter of plugging in the pieces:

- Misunderstood market selection: Young, hip, disaffected urbanites in the top ten TV markets.
- Misunderstood media: "Alternative" publications such as the *Village Voice, Chicago Reader,* and *LA Weekly.* As for television, it was *Saturday Night Live,* period.
- Misunderstood event marketing: Rock promotions.

The Dr Pepper selected prospects were defined by media choices. Media dictated what they wore, where to eat, and when to move to the next neighborhood. Their media help to reinforce their ethics and allegiance to the precepts of their crowd. Thus our strategy was to play the "misunderstood" theme to the audiences of the *Village Voice* and the *Chicago Reader* and *Saturday Night Live.* We had Dr Pepper drinkers hiding in closets or surrounded by cases of Dr P in a room decorated with Dr P memorabilia. In short, we took what our research told us was the public perception of the brand

and threw it back at them—but with the message that something (or someone) could be misunderstood but still be part of a group.

It's important to point out that, although selective marketing could accurately position Dr Pepper as "America's Most Misunderstood Soft Drink," without just the right tone of voice, just the right amount of irreverence, just the right touch of offhanded sarcasm, it would not have rung true and succeeded. Achieving those nuances required developing an insider's understanding of a targeted market segment, and Y&R management went about it in the most logical way: They composed the creative team of members who fit the selected target profile—essentially market insiders—and put them to work on a brand that wanted to be the insider's soft drink. It worked.

By developing an insider's understanding of their target market's sensitivities through the work of Y&R's downtown creatives, the uptown "suits" in account management were able to convey the client's product as both different and better than the competition: an alternative for the alternative culture. Especially with a target customer who considers him- or herself outside the mainstream, a selective marketing campaign has two goals:

> **SMART Marketing:**
>
> Sometimes the market segment is you. When that's the case, remember that self-analysis is helpful, but don't stop there. Talk to enough other market representatives to find the full range of values consumers identify with.

1. Ensure that the consumer understands the sales message.

2. Convince the consumer that you understand his or her needs.

In the case of Dr Pepper, the selected consumers came to believe that "the misunderstood soft drink" was a better, or at least different, way to quench their thirst, and they felt it validated them as individuals. Remember that in 1972 people who were born in 1948 were 24 years old—baby boomers. The counterculture that we were targeting was one of the largest segments of American society. These former hippies were misunderstood as they graduated from college, entered the workforce, and came back from the war in Vietnam. Dr Pepper was also "misunderstood," so both the target market and the soft drink were seeking acceptance. As each of our ads and commercials stressed, "If people would only try us, they'd like us." Our market segment's sentiments exactly. As that empathetic chord resonated, Dr Pepper began to move into the newly acquired markets of New York, Chicago, and Los Angeles. Within eight years, Dr Pepper became a national brand and took the number three spot in the soft drink wars from 7UP (which had been put there by J. Walter Thompson, Chicago's "Uncola" campaign years earlier).

THE TIMES THEY ARE A'CHANGIN'

The danger inherent in targeting young, hip consumers is losing sight of the fact that as the consumers mature, their wants and needs change. Simply, the hipper the advertising, the more quickly it becomes outdated. So, in 1975, Y&R realized it was time to test for the targeted segment's current needs and wants. "Endless consumer dialogue," we call it at SMART. At Y&R, it was time to put a new team to work on what had essentially become a "new" target market.

It was determined that the target market for Dr Pepper had expanded, as had the audience for *Saturday Night Live*. A broader audience required a broader positioning. And so the next phase of the Dr Pepper expansion campaign was to create parodies of great films. This go-around, money was no object. Creative supervisor Dominick Rosetti's budgets exceeded the cost of some of the most popular feature films of the time, such as *Easy-Rider* or *One Flew Over the Cuckoo's Nest*. It was considered well worth the expense to edge 7UP out of the number three spot in domestic soft drink sales. Ironically, Dr Pepper, once so misunderstood, began to enjoy mainstream recognition. Its fame peaked with the now famous "I'm a Pepper, You're a Pepper" campaign, which had the whole nation humming the refrain. Goodbye, selective marketing. Hello, mass marketing.

Since then, the Peppers have come and gone, and the brand has changed hands and is now owned by Schweppes Cadbury. The soft drink went back to its southern roots and, as of this writing, "Just What the Dr Ordered" is its campaign. Perhaps the biggest testament to the success of the Dr Pepper consumer franchise is the recent word that Coca-Cola is diligently working on a Dr Pepper–type soft drink.

Select Marketing Lessons

The most important lesson to take from the Dr Pepper experience is to stay abreast of changes—in your selected market, in the creative team working on the project, in society as a whole. All can signal the need to reevaluate a select marketing campaign. Selective marketing is one proven method of keeping up with, and when possible, staying ahead of, consumer changes, but it's not the only way.

When selective marketing techniques are employed to expand a customer base and they succeed to the point at which the select market becomes the mass market (as happened with Dr Pepper), it's time to switch to more traditional mass-marketing strategies. Selective marketing is not intended to be a replacement for other, more traditional methods. Sometimes, the right decision for a client is not to use, or to stop using, selective marketing techniques.

For Dr Pepper, that time came when the values and the influence of the select market grew to the point of being those of the majority of domestic consumers. The important thing to keep in mind is that the conditions that make a selective market or series of selective markets grow to mass-market proportions will always be external and therefore beyond the control of the marketer. Dr Pepper could not inspire the alienation felt by those it selected to market to; Dr Pepper could only empathize with that alienation and use it to build a bridge to an ultimate consumer relationship.

10

TENDER LOVING HEALTH CARE:
Treating Patients as Individuals

for Midway Hospital Medical Center

- **Market:** Diverse, select populations, each with specific health care requirements.

- **Marketing Challenge:** Demonstrate that a smaller medical center had advantages over larger, more well-known competitors in the area, thereby giving it greater market share.

- **Marketing Solution:** Conduct multiselective marketing outreach programs, each directed to a different segment of the health care marketplace.

- **Outcome:** Midway Hospital Medical Center continues to meet the financial objectives of a for-profit medical institution by serving the wide spectrum of needs posed by its diverse publics. Its CEO and business development managers are now in charge of multiple hospitals for the second largest national hospital network in the nation, Tenet HealthSystem.

Cultural diversity and economic disparity are facts of life for Midway Hospital Medical Center, in Los Angeles, California. An estimated 1.7 million people make up Midway Hospital's primary service area, which, within a one-mile radius of the center, includes Koreatown, West Hollywood, gang-dominated South Central L.A., Beverly Hills, and Century City. Furthermore, this human landscape is ever changing: Ethnic communities form from Korea, Persia, Ethiopia, El Salvador, and the former Soviet Union; former orthodox and reformed Jewish neighborhoods become Persian and African-American, while traditional African-American communities house more young Hispanic and Anglo families on the block. Hong Kong Chinese are the anticipated next wave in Midway's service corridor. Clearly, such population diversity seriously affects how a service-based organization like Midway Hospital Medical Center conducts business and markets itself and its staff.

> **SMART Marketing:**
>
> Managers whose products or services are dependent upon several diverse populations are only as effective as their ability to be open-minded and stay informed.

Therefore, it was the goal of the hospital's managers to address each and every one of those market segments individually, for each has its unique culture, values, fears, and needs. Wisely, the director of business development, Greg Madsen, realized that Midway's services could not be promoted effectively using traditional mass-market strategies. Midway chose to promote its programs by marketing its various specialty centers (for example, urology, AIDS, plastic surgery, infertility) to identified potential consumers for those practices in the surrounding zip codes that make up Midway's area of dominant influence. This is prime real estate for selective marketing.

PREVENTIVE MARKETING

Probably no industry in the 1990s has been more controversial and unsettled than the health care industry. At odds are politicians, health care providers, insurance companies, and the public. Most significant of the changes wrought by the evolution in this field has been the advent and widespread use of HMOs. To adjust to the changes, Midway focuses its activities on aligning and organizing medical groups and physician alliances. Its business development department then approaches an HMO for a contract. Once the contract is awarded, Midway must inform the public of its alliance with the HMO, to encourage patronage. This is the future of health care, and Midway intends to make sure it provides the best service for the health care consumer while integrating the new and sometimes complicated insurance plans.

Midway's CEO John Fenton understood early in the health care controversy that the notion of product differential becomes more meaningful once the proper selective marketing techniques are applied. In this way, Midway Hospital believes it can secure a dominant share of the health care marketplace in its sphere by marketing segment by segment, in contrast to its major competitor in the area, the world-renowned Cedars-Sinai. Cedars-Sinai may be perceived as a great hospital, but if a consumer wants a specific practitioner (as a result of advertising), that consumer will accept and embrace Midway as the delivery mechanism.

In the Shadow of a Giant
Today, Midway Hospital is a SMART client. Brought in by Fenton in 1993 to work with Greg Madsen, SMART began a practice group–by–practice group selective marketing analysis of the hospital's core constituencies. Madsen believed that the services provided by Midway were well suited to the various groups the hospital seeks to serve. He realized that each of these groups approaches health care from a very different vantage point. Some define health care as catastrophic care; others define it as preventive care. Together with Madsen and his business development team, SMART's job was to determine the best way to emphasize certain aspects of those services to make them con-

gruent with the cultural values of the populations Midway was determined to reach.

As part of SMART's preliminary research, I asked Madsen, "What advantage does selective marketing give you over Cedars-Sinai promotional activities?" He said, "People want not only quality care but the tender loving care that is offered by a smaller neighborhood facility like Midway. We are more closely aligned with our neighborhoods. We're more involved with our community. Cedars is a great competitor . . . but they can't do what we do here. We are warmer, friendlier, easier to understand." What better definition of selective marketing could there be?

SMART lost no time in jumping on the opportunity to market these previously unheralded advantages. One of the ways SMART accomplished this was by instituting a direct-mail campaign to pre-register the medical statistics of the residents of five zip-code areas surrounding the hospital. This LifeLine Program helped Beverly Hills residents cut through the red tape and afforded non-English-speaking residents the ability to not be held up by translation problems at admittance in emergency situations.

For the reproductive medicine practices, we targeted couples battling infertility by advertising seminars on the subject in the 12 English and foreign language weekly newspapers that serve Midway's trading area as well as the west-side edition of the *Los Angeles Times.* We also utilized talk radio for this delicate subject and got an ABC radio talk show host to do an on-air testimonial about how she became pregnant after being treated by a Midway infertility program. For another infertility program, we utilized commercials on the area's local cable channel. The more localized the media to Midway's trading area, the better.

By communicating to Beverly Hills residents that Midway offers greater privacy, less bureaucracy, and therefore smoother, quicker registration procedures than Cedars-Sinai, we were able to convince them of Midway's convenience. To quote Madsen: "Being able to control your environment is important to a patient—not being a number; having a face. Midway prides itself on not just assigning people a number and saying wait in this line for three hours and then you'll get some services. We see them right now, quickly. We greet them with a handshake. People enjoy that." SMART set out to custom-tailor such benefits to every one of the selected market segments.

The staff at Midway believed that being in the shadow of world-famous Cedars-Sinai presented an exciting, albeit somewhat daunting, challenge. They knew that there were many people in the Beverly Hills environment who would choose Midway if they were made aware of its many services and personal approach, so SMART went to work to ensure that more people did just that. We found out what we had to sell and whom we had to sell it to; we disregarded the rest. This is how we broke down Midway's select target markets, along with its respective target service:

- The Immune Suppression Unit to the HIV/AIDS community
- The Prostate Institute to older African-American and Korean men
- The Estheticare Cosmetic Plastic Surgery Unit to the upmarket enclaves of southern California and the business community
- The Infertility Practice to upper-middle-income couples
- A highly confidential plastic surgery center dedicated to the special needs of the performing arts community

To enhance customer interest, SMART utilized several meaningful, and in some cases very different, outreach methodologies, also very specifically targeted; for example:

- Ads in Persian magazines featuring Persian babies, written *in Persian,* to promote a noted Persian infertility specialist.

- A tour of the Midway Immune Suppression Unit for White House AIDS czar Christine Gebbie.

- Because the Latino population has a higher incidence of diabetes, Midway developed a diabetes program with Hispanic doctors, then advertised that program to the Mexican, Salvadoran, Nicaraguan, and Guatemalan communities.

- We supported our ER early admissions program with bus benches.

- A Heartburn Center billboard was placed on the main traffic artery between Beverly Hills and downtown Los Angeles financial and fashion centers.

- Because Midway is blocks away from the Wilshire business corridor, we advertised plastic surgery for men in the *L.A. Business Journal.*

- Taking into account the spicy foods enjoyed by many Hispanic cultures, we promoted a stomach pain program in Spanish on bus benches and in Spanish language newspapers.

- Because the Midway trading area covers a large enclave of retirees, we utilized local giveaway newspapers to tout an incontinence program.

HITTING A MOVING TARGET

The most challenging aspect of the selective marketing initiative for Midway Hospital proved to be deploying it amid the continuous growth and the incalculable degree of change in the health care industry—it was like trying to hit a moving target.

Madsen helped us to stay in touch with the new health care movement to help us best direct our selective marketing plans for the hospital. He explained that the hospital's efforts necessarily went toward aligning itself with other "partners," whether they be physician groups, other hospitals, or HMOs, and then developing strategies that take their products and the hospital's and target a certain community. In the past, the hospital would simply develop a program, name a medical director for that program, and market that program to the community that would use it. Today, the process is much more complex.

Focused Care

To stay competitive, the hospital staff and management had to familiarize themselves with new interpersonal skills, social values, and performance criteria. And an important source of input for the hospital to stay in touch with its multicultural client base was focus groups composed of members of the various communities, in which hospital staff fielded very general and very specific questions to try to understand their neighbors' perceptions of Midway. The purpose of this early research was to determine not only exactly who Midway's neighbors were, but what they believed Midway's roles and responsibilities were as a hospital in west Los Angeles.

This research brought a lot of insight and assistance to Midway management in charting the hospital's future direction. We learned that in the health care industry, perhaps more than in any other service profession, word-of-mouth information distribution is prevalent—people refer friends and family to a doctor they like; they share pleasant or unpleasant hospital experiences; they discuss the frustrations of navigating the maze that is the insurance industry. In short, word-of-mouth "press" can mean the difference between success

SMART Marketing:

The importance of ongoing focus groups in determining a market segment's attitude regarding a product or service should never be underestimated. They can help you identify and isolate potentially overlooked problem areas or even crisis situations before they become overt.

and failure to a hospital whose client base is made up of several diverse and tightly knit communities. Case in point: Midway both serves and employs a large number of people active in the gay community, which helps to promote the values of the hospital to others in that market segment. Consequently, if a person has AIDS and needs a referral, he or she is more likely to feel more comfortable choosing Midway, which, in conjunction with its superb Immune Suppression facility, has built a reputation for being sensitive to the special fears and needs of the gay community. As Madsen says: "It is important to have people that work in the hospital reflect the people we serve. It's a natural link."

WHERE THE BUCK STOPS

Unquestionably, one of the primary tenets of selective marketing is that an organization become as knowledgeable as possible about the target market. And when marketing for the health care industry, that means determining how clients will pay for their treatment, because their health care choices are often based in great part on their insurance plans. So in addition to identifying Midway Hospital Medical Center's various select markets, in conjunction with the business development department, we defined its three core business segments:

1. Clients using MediCal, a Medicaid-funded program
2. Commercial clients, those people paying for insurance through a health plan at work or on an individual basis
3. Senior clients receiving Medicare benefits

Ultimately, all three of these groups will go into so-called managed care programs. For example, a person eligible for Medicare benefits can select an HMO. SMART's goal was to market Midway in such a way that the Medicare patient would select an HMO partnered with Midway. Using selective marketing techniques and a variety of strategies and executions, we achieved our primary objective of education. By educating each selected market, providing community resources for the people in it, and providing benefits they need and don't have, Midway is more likely to attract patients to its facility and to the medical practices with which it is affiliated.

SELECTIVE MARKETING FOR THE LONG TERM

One of our jobs as selective marketers is to prepare organizations to deal with the results and the future of their selective marketing efforts. At Midway, this was both an internal as well as an external task:

- Internally, staff had to become more knowledgeable about and sensitive to the various market segments and their requirements, demands, and expectations.

- Externally, Midway had to overcome what Madsen believed was an inherent public distrust of advertising, especially in the medical profession, although he acknowledged that "ads still work," because they give the public information about available services.

After a program has been initiated, the client must be aware that it is still necessary to monitor its success. To that end, Midway has instituted full-page patient satisfaction surveys to be completed by emergency room patients, inpatients, and outpatients. The hospital also surveys each of its physicians, because they often hear patient feedback. Finally, the hospital bases its performance appraisals of department managers on the results of those patient satisfaction surveys, so that each department has an incentive to provide a high level of patient satisfaction.

As a result of this use of selective marketing by the Business Development Department at Midway Hospital Medical Center, a 50-year-old medical facility that was marginally profitable turned the corner to viability. Patient census figures have risen and the hospital has absorbed nearby Westside Hospital and been acquired by Tenet HealthSystem, the second largest private hospital chain in the nation.

Select Marketing Lessons

The most important selective marketing principle is that every audience is made up of *individuals,* and though it would be ludicrous to try and promote a product or service to one person at a time, selective marketing does enable a greater degree of intimacy than traditional mass-marketing techniques, which essentially shoot a promotional arrow into the air and hope it hits a probable client. In no business or industry is treating people as individuals more important than in the health care industry, where the customers are either patients or the friends and family of patients. This customer base is highly vulnerable—emotionally, financially, and physically. These customers must be treated as having names and faces, not just as forms and ailments. Selective marketing enables the kind of sensitive approach it takes to engender trust for health care givers and centers. And that trust can be an important advantage over competition that still regards its clients as numbers. Selective marketing strategies also make it easier to stay abreast of the ongoing changes in this or any other volatile field.

11

COMMUNITY TIES:

The Multicultural Marketing of a Political Program

for the Los Angeles Business Revitalization Center

- **Market:** Inner-city small businesspeople in Los Angeles, California.

- **Marketing Challenge:** Following widespread rioting, small business owners were left adrift among the ruins, with no information readily available about the government relief programs that would help them to begin the rebuilding process.

- **Marketing Solution:** Establish a well-placed "revitalization" center and launch outreach campaigns to hardest-hit groups.

- **Outcome:** Small businesspeople were given the aid and encouragement they needed to rebuild—with a minimum of red tape.

When the smoke had cleared following the widespread rioting and looting that tore apart Los Angeles, California, in 1993, it was obvious to everyone that most of the damage had been wreaked on small businesses. And of that group, the number of businesses destroyed that were owned by members of the city's Korean community (the largest enclave of

Korean Americans in North America) was higher than most. It was the sorry finale to long-standing friction between Korean merchants and their African-American customers in South Central Los Angeles and had been foreshadowed by shootings and isolated store burnings. Following the strategic firebombing of strip malls in the area, where many of those businesses owned by Koreans were decimated to their foundations, all hell had broken loose.

In the uneasy calm that settled in the immediate aftermath of the riots, California's Republican governor, Pete Wilson, promised all business owners whose establishments had been damaged or destroyed by the flames that the government would help them to rebuild. His plan was to institute what he called a Business Revitalization Center (BRC), dedicated to easing the way for all factions of the mixed community to start anew.

But, true to the nature of political appeasement plans, this one, too, would have to be thrashed out among the powers that be. In the year it took to pass the legislation, Los Angeles simmered in its political hotbed:

- African-American community organizations were protesting against state liquor licenses being reissued to Korean liquor stores.

- Across the street from City Hall, Korean civic groups held daily demonstrations demanding reparations as promised from the government for losses suffered at the hands of rioters.

- The insurance industry had announced that a large percentage of claims filed by merchants affected by the riot were considered fraudulent.

- Allegedly, following the riots, certain members of the Korean community had been given advance notice of special disaster loans, by officers of their local banks, and the information spread so fast that Korean civic organizations began to hold seminars to help applicants fill out their loan applications. Conversely, in the African-American community bank branches were being accused of not processing applications or of discouraging applicants. By the time most African Americans' loans were approved, the loan pool had been depleted.

SMART Marketing:

When promoting a social marketing message, know the infrastructure of your target audience. Though sometimes seemingly out of the mainstream, ethnic and cultural groups often maintain well-organized and tightly knit networks, whose influence and aid selective marketers must seek.

By the time Wilson had gotten the go-ahead for his plan, small businesspeople were furious with both the private sector, which they had perceived as dropping the ball on fair play, and the state, which seemed to them to be dragging its feet. More than ever, it was incumbent upon Wilson to successfully implement the Business Revitalization Center—and in a hurry.

PROMISES TO KEEP

To ensure a level playing field, the policymakers on the governor's project were black, Asian, and Hispanic; going in, everyone knew that, to work, this had to be an equal opportunity campaign. The Business Revitalization Center was to be the state's red-tape cutter and expediter for riot-weary small businesspeople struggling to rebuild; it would be a centrally located facility where they could access representatives of each of the government agencies involved in the reconstruction process.

Although for years, Los Angeles had been a Democratic stronghold, Pete Wilson was the state's third Republican governor in a row. He had forged his career on being a friend of small business. To turn his revitalization goal from "paper promise" into a fully functional program, the governor had to rely upon Tom Sayles, his secretary of business, housing, and transportation, and the offices of the L.A. Economic Development Corporation (EDC). The governor's team had 30 days to make it happen in hostile territory. The pressure was on because the one-year deadline for the governor's promised aid to South Central Los Angeles businesses was less than a month away. With national attention focused on Los Angeles and the governor's political ambitions, a broken promise was not in Wilson's game plan.

SMART Politics

Exactly one year to the date of Governor Wilson's promise to the devastated constituents of Los Angeles, on the recommendation of multicultural marketing specialists Muse, Cordero & Chen, SMART was given the assignment of spreading the news to Korean, Hispanic, and African-American businesspeople in Los Angeles that help was going to be made available. Governor Wilson's 30-day deadline became our 30-day deadline: It was July 4, 1993, and the BRC was scheduled to open July 22, 1993.

SMART surveyed the political, cultural, and media opportunities and recommended that Governor Wilson's Business Revitalization Center utilize three selective marketing programs to communicate one message clearly and effectively to business owners in the affected areas of Los Angeles. That message: The state, county, city, and federal governments have joined forces to help your business grow.

The race was on. Over the long holiday weekend, we set about defining the pros and cons of our status, an essential task when on a tight deadline. The pros were:

• Our target audience was already identified, and we knew their problems and needs.

- We knew the message we had to impart.
- Our "product" was given an ideal location, in the brand-new Baldwin Hills/Crenshaw Mall, in the heart of riot-torn South Central Los Angeles, thanks to developer Alexander Hagin.

The cons were:

- The political community was in upheaval following the swearing-in of a new mayor. We would have to maneuver our selective marketing program through a political minefield. Mayor Richard J. Riordan, although a Republican, was not an ally of Governor Wilson and, in effect, had been one of the governor's most vocal critics.
- While juggling political hot potatoes, we had to somehow convey the image that Governor Wilson's Business Revitalization Center was an oasis of total cooperation between state, county, city, and federal governments.
- Previous "one-stop" business permit centers had achieved only marginal success. Pessimism was rampant.

Fortunately for SMART, the tactical systems at the EDC were faster at setting up offices than the city's, county's, and state's abilities to resist the changes brought on by consolidation. Also, the office of Secretary Sayles had the considerable clout of CalTrans (the California Department of Transportation) to count on if push came to shove. The California State Business, Transportation, and Housing Agency (BT&H) staff worked with each of the BRC partner agencies to finalize financial and personnel responsibilities. Because BT&H interacted with county, city, and federal agencies and provided services (and funding) for many of the agencies involved, its influence in motivating slow-moving bureaucracies was considerable.

With the facilities and government agency coordination being handled expertly by the EDC and Sayles's office, SMART was left the formidable task of building the government's media bridge to the Hispanic, Korean, and African-American business communities in fewer than ten days after developing and producing the creative materials for print, outdoor, and radio advertising in English, Spanish, and Korean.

One of the tenets of selective marketing is the process of learning as we go. It is critical when defining the values and motivations of the markets we seek to influence. A selective marketing program may find, postlaunch, that it has to influence many subsegments of the population, in addition to the primary target market, to create the proper perception in the decision-making apparatus of the selected consumer. For example, to influence African-American, Korean, and Hispanic businesspeople, we had to influence their churches, their civic and cultural organizations, and their financial institutions. This was the result of the considerable lack of credibility that government agencies had with our targeted audiences.

In social selective marketing programs, perception is everything, as business, community, and political factions vie for press coverage and the right to be right. The result is that marketers tasked with disseminating information or promoting a message may find that the way something is said or written is more important than the actual content; that is, function follows form. The message must be expressed equally to each of the target populations. In the case of reaching the warring factions of Los Angeles with Governor Wilson's information about the Business Revitalization Center, we decided against using slang or humor because such idiomatic executions generally do not translate accurately and/or tastefully across language and cultural barriers.

SMART Marketing:

When using social selective marketing programs that must address a multicultural target population, it may be wise to launch multilingual campaigns simultaneously, to avoid the appearance of bias.

Time, too, became a factor, because to win the commitment of every state, county, and city entity whose support we needed for the opening event, each of those factions expected the right to sign off on the campaign—that is, to approve the campaign.

It was Jai Henderson, the newly appointed executive director of the Business Revitalization Center, who came up with the campaign slogan, which was short, simple, and to the point: "We Help Your Business Grow." Henderson had the political clout necessary to push that message through in the short time allotted. She had been recruited from the powerful Rebuild L.A. task force, her husband was involved with Governor Wilson's campaign, and she was Mayor Riordan's next-door neighbor.

> **SMART Marketing:**
>
> When dealing with political entities, factor in additional time constraints imposed by the levels of hierarchical approval mechanisms.

The Price of Politics
With the creative considerations out of the way, we could deal with the logistics of approval, revisions, extensions in newspaper, direct mail, outdoor advertising, and radio. Twelve executions in three languages had to be approved by the appropriate authorities in time to make a closing date for opening-week media. But as the deadline loomed, the EDC stopped us dead in our tracks. Not only were we expected to develop three separate but equal selective marketing programs, we were also expected to secure a percentage of the media on a donated or pro bono basis. Late in the game, the state had discovered the practice of value-added media and production services and was determined to get its fair share. Working with EDC, SMART set out to put the arm on our already taxed media and production resources. (SMART's pro bono contribution to the cause was the development of a first-year marketing plan.)

Shandra Shah of the EDC, along with SMART and media buying service Vitt Media, solicited two-for-one deals from each media outlet. This means that for every billboard, ad insertion, and radio spot the state bought, it expected a second to be donated as a public service by the media. In general, the media were glad to comply, and we were able to provide four times their spending level in communications value to the BRC.

SMART Marketing:

Maintaining an accurate cost accounting system is never more important than when doing business with a government agency. No matter how tight the deadline, know at all times where the client's money is going.

One final glitch threatened our chances of making the deadline. At a meeting to review status, we realized that one critical element had been left out of the mix: No one had thought to secure bona fide success stories to which the Business Revitalization Center could lay claim once the public began utilizing its services. This, of course, meant that the BRC had to be operational one week earlier than planned to process referrals from the state, city, county, and federal agencies involved. This was tricky because of the "no leaks" policy of notifying the public in unison. A Korean, an African-American, and a Hispanic business were selected by Jai Henderson and Tom Sayles to go through the BRC system 24 hours before the office was officially open to the public, so that when Governor Wilson arrived for the grand opening he could meet with them and get firsthand feedback from business-people who had seen the BRC in action. Without proof of the center's efficacy, the governor ran the risk of the local press identifying the center with previous failed attempts to pull together state, county, city, and federal efforts to aid victims of civil unrest.

A "shakedown cruise" was in order, to prove beyond a doubt that this program would indeed work. A key point in this preopening run-through period was the determination of whether these various government agencies could, in fact, work together under one roof. Could bureaucratic red tape be done away with? Could the team approach be used by several different permit-issuing branches of local government? Could the promise of "one-stop" government services be delivered? What had been the problems encountered in previous efforts to streamline the activities of city, state, and county agencies by getting them to operate under one roof? Now SMART was charged with determining whether the "product" offered by the BRC could be delivered as promised in our advertising. By enlisting the help of each participating agency to provide test candidates for the preopening trial run, we found the glitches in the system and attended to their speedy repair by pulling together all of the representatives of the agencies involved and hammering out workable solutions. We were soon confident that, come opening day, the BRC would be able to deliver on Governor Wilson's ambitious promise.

Remarkably, Governor Wilson's Business Revitalization Center opened on time, and the "triplet" spots ran within minutes of each other on all the ethnic broadcast outlets in Los Angeles. The governor had delivered on his promise to get state, county, city, and even federal agencies to work together to help business rebuild in the riot-torn areas, and SMART, through savvy selective marketing techniques, had delivered a campaign that enabled him to renew the public's faith in government.

We had researched the problems that led up to the riots. We had researched the problems that occurred after the riots to those who were trying to rebuild their businesses. We had researched the attitudes and opinions of the government employees charged with delivering services to these businesses. We had researched where and why those government agencies had failed to deliver those services. We had researched what the net effect of this failure had been on the victims of the riots. SMART was then able to share this information with each of the many factions involved with the BRC so that they might better understand the mind-sets of each of our selected markets.

It was the findings of these research probes that lead to the preopening testing of BRC's systems and procedures to ensure that there would be no foul-ups to generate negative publicity that might counteract our selective marketing efforts in each of our targeted communities. This is a perfect example of how selective marketing techniques and procedures can be utilized in *advance* of a product or service introduction to help ensure a successful launch.

And the Business Revitalization Center was a success. Within its first six months of operations, the BRC assisted more than 500 businesses with zoning variances and state DBE certification, as well as taxation, permits, and building code information for which they otherwise would have had to wait in countless lines at city, county, and state offices spread throughout the vast L.A. basin.

Select Marketing Lessons

SMART learned several lessons while putting together the social selective marketing campaign for Governor Pete Wilson in the early 1990s—some of them the hard way. Therefore, the goal of this case study is to introduce and alert other marketing specialists to the factors particular to working with political entities as clients:

- If a political or campaign promise is the basis for the social marketing program, count on longer approval times and higher degrees of scrutiny from the key policy influencers and opposition media.

- If your selective marketing program has to influence various subsegments of a target audience, *perception*, rather than form or content, may prove to be your most important goal. Such programs must be perceived as fair, equal, and sensitive to each group's needs and issues.

- Although money is an issue in any marketing campaign, and marketers must always keep close tabs on spending, particularly with social or political groups, money is a touchy topic. Keep in mind that this money is often—usually—taxpayer money, so essentially you must answer to more than just the client sitting across the conference room table.

- The backing and clout of political influencers is important, and often necessary, to the success of a socially directed campaign, but it, too, must be used wisely and sensitively. Sometimes clout is perceived as bullying by certain factions of the target audience.

12

PHONING HOME:

Changing Hispanic Calling Patterns

for AT&T

- **Market:** Hispanic families in America with strong ties to their countries of origin.

- **Marketing Challenge:** Convince the select market that AT&T could address their specific needs and calling concerns if they would call after 6 P.M.

- **Marketing Solution:** Demonstrate via television advertising that AT&T understood and was accommodating the needs of Hispanic customers by informing them of "better" times to call home.

- **Outcome:** AT&T was able to redirect Hispanic calling patterns and thus answer the Hispanic consumer concerns regarding the problem of overburdened long-distance lines.

n 1987, AT&T began to aggressively teach its managers the wisdom of selective marketing as a way to more effectively reach its increasingly diversified consumer population. The communications giant was one of the first of the Fortune 500 to set the stage for the use of targeted, or segmented, marketing. Beginning with its early award-winning African-American consumer market commercials in the 1970s, AT&T became a dominant force in understanding the wisdom of speaking *with* its customers, not *at* them.

It was no surprise, then, that when AT&T wanted to reach out to one of the largest of these diverse consumer groups—the approximately 33 million Spanish-speaking Americans—it made the choice to use selective marketing techniques to get the level of insight that was needed to really speak their language, literally and figuratively. To compel Hispanic customers to apply the AT&T line of products and services to address their needs, AT&T staff first had to familiarize themselves with the dynamics—the reality—of life in this country for this large, but somewhat insular, consumer group.

CROSSING THE LANGUAGE BARRIER

AT&T retained Bermudez & Associates to teach its staff the "right" Spanish to use in marketing to the Hispanic communities of los Estados Unidos. Bermudez president Jim Golightly was a career telco man, a seasoned executive who left the security of Ma Bell to join forces with Eduardo Bermudez, whom I had first met when he worked at Foote, Cone, Belding in Chicago. Their $2-million Hispanic ad agency was booming. Bermudez subsequently called in SMART to help his team target its efforts more efficiently. Their expertise was the Hispanic marketplace; ours was selective marketing: It was the ideal match to take on the challenge presented by AT&T. The long-distance carrier was having big problems with the sheer volume of calls between the United States and Mexico. It had to try and separate the flow of business and personal traffic into the overburdened switching facilities in Mexico City.

Reality Check

With the team in place, work could begin. And the first task (as it always is in selective marketing) was to become fluent with the values and perceptions of AT&T's Hispanic customers. The AT&T marketing teams immersed themselves in the latest trends and events of importance to Hispanic customers. We conducted studies and focus groups in five select markets throughout the Southwest to determine consumer attitudes and reactions, to evolve a knowledge base of the Hispanic family structure in the United States.

The purpose of these studies was to determine how much resistance would be met in the attempt to get our target audience to change their calling patterns. During a 90-day period we interviewed 800 people in Los Angeles, San Diego, Phoenix, Tucson, Albuquerque, San Antonio, Dallas/Fort Worth, and Houston. In these interviews we asked how often they called, during what time periods they called, how long their conversations generally lasted, what family members usually initiated the calls, and which family members received the calls in Mexico. We utilized local market research contractors in each city to recruit respondents and we flew in moderators to conduct each focus group.

As a result of this extensive probe into the lifestyles, calling patterns, and attitudes toward the phone system of the target market, we were able to gain tremendous insight into the reality of life for Hispanics living in the United States. The following is a sample of these insights:

- Home, for many of these people, is a long-distance phone call away, but staying in touch by phone with faraway relatives is a big expense, because telephone ownership in many of these immigrants' countries of origin is not as widespread as in the

United States. Many Hispanics must rely on neighbors or businesses with phones in their homelands; this means they have to place most of their calls during the day—the most costly time to do so—to accommodate business hours or as a courtesy to a private party. Hence, the large volume of daytime calls.

- A significant percentage of immigrants from Mexico and Central America live in "cluster households," that is, households composed of more than one family, which share resources, expenses, work, child care, and more. This infrastructure enables them to more easily establish credit, provide education for their children, and eventually, bring more of their relatives to the United States, but it also has a tendency to isolate them from the community at large. Hence, the longer duration of personal calls.

- Many in the Hispanic communities have a deep, underlying mistrust for "La Telefónica," bred of suffering under governments that believe in invasion of privacy as a way to control the people—where wiretapping was either known or believed to be widespread; therefore, we could expect our market to be resistant to our message without a clear personal benefit.

In short, many Hispanics' experience with telephone service was anything but positive. Nevertheless, they were also well aware of the importance of having long-distance service now that they were in the United States. Not only was it their primary means for staying in touch with their friends and families, a phone bill was also an important piece of paper—proof of residence and stability—to have as they struggled to establish their lives in America. In lieu of a driver's license, work visa, or green card, a phone bill was often enough to enable them to get electric service, vaccinations for their children, employment, and much more. Phone service, for them, was not a luxury; it was a necessity. Our selective marketing mission, then, was to convince Hispanic consumers that AT&T could help satisfy their need to communicate with loved ones in their homelands more cheaply if they would consider changing their calling patterns.

Answering Questions with Questions

But first we had to dig deeper, because the answers to our research questions led to questions we had to ask ourselves:

1. Could the selected customer afford the cost of long-distance service? If not, would lower costs motivate a change in calling times?

2. Was the selected customer creditworthy enough to warrant this special marketing effort?

3. How could we find the answers to the first and second questions without offending the selected customer?

A second round of research gave us the answers we needed. Long-distance charges were a considerable burden, so lower rates were a definite incentive to change calling patterns. Not only were our targeted consumers creditworthy, they had combined family incomes that were in excess of their Anglo counterparts and their practice of living in "cluster households" eventually leads to several billing accounts at one address, making them superconsumers of telephone services. To gain the answers to the more sensitive questions, we utilized surrogate interviewers (church and community organizations) rather than standard research contractors.

At first, the AT&T marketing teams were not very clear about their selective marketing criteria. Usage surveys and consumer research had helped to identify which cultural segments of the population indexed highest in long-distance calling pattern. And AT&T was convinced that the cluster-family infrastructure was a perfect application for the services it provided. But our research also revealed that there were many subsegments of the so-called Hispanic market. We had to become mindful of the fact that Hispanic means Mexican Americans, Cuban Americans, Puerto Ricans, Dominicans, Salvadorans, Guatemalans, and Nicaraguans—each of which could be considered as a subsegment, because each had

- Significant self-interest media

- Viable political, cultural, or trade representation

- Capable product or service distribution channels

- Financial viability and stability

> **SMART Marketing:**
>
> Selective marketing begins and ends with research, but research is only the foundation for a creative strategy.

Unfortunately, the creative objective was not geared to speak to each subsegment; to do so would have been cost-prohibitive. Research is always key in such dilemmas, but it is only the foundation for meaningful and compelling creative executions in print and broadcast media. Without a well-defined, well-conceived creative strategy, the research is meaningless.

SPANISH SPOKEN HERE

Though necessary for the client, trying to accommodate the many dialects of Spanish-speaking customers made the creative aspect of the selective marketing strategy much more complex. And it was SMART's role to manage the creative implementation of the program in tandem with Bermudez creative directors, Fernando Tomayo and Anita Santiago.

Since long-distance rates were determined by our research to be a prime motivator in influencing the calling patterns of our selected market, AT&T opened the campaign with a salvo of print ads that gave price comparisons for daytime calls versus evening calls. These ads were run in Spanish-language newspapers that served the Mexican, Nicaraguan, and Salvadoran communities in the Southwest and West.

But the research had told us more. We learned that these calls were special events in the lives of our targeted audiences and those they were calling. In matters of lifestyle and emotion, nothing sells like television, and Spanish-language television is no exception. By positioning the long-distance phone call as an occasion worthy of planning for, our television campaign could dramatize a series of these special occasions in which all the members of the family could participate if they made the effort to plan for the calls in advance. Naturally, the best times to call were when the kids were home from school and Dad was home from work. The early evening hours were positioned as the ideal time for the entire family to enjoy the call and have a better chance of the call going through. We utilized situations that cut across the cultural boundaries of our selected market's subsegments. A new girlfriend, a birthday greeting, lovers trying to connect with each other—all transcended cultural barriers.

SMART Marketing:

To be successful, a foreign language creative endeavor requires fluency in the native tongue of the target market, coupled with a sensitivity to the culture of the foreign speakers. Idioms and slang are not directly translatable; they can cause misunderstandings or be offensive.

Producing a television commercial is always fraught with problems and frustration. In the case of the AT&T campaign, our first problem was that the company hired to shoot the 30-second spots claimed that none of the commercials were written "to time." This was not surprising, considering the translation process we had to follow to get these spots through AT&T client and legal approval:

1. The scripts were written in Spanish.
2. The scripts were translated into English for client changes.
3. The scripts were translated back into Spanish for broadcast.
4. An as-recorded script was translated back into English for final client approval.

Each script went through this grueling and time-consuming process, and I was assigned the responsibility of making the scripts fit the time frame. This I ultimately accomplished by shaving seconds or second fragments off wherever I could—in one case, overlapping dialogue; in another, changing an actor's response to a gesture. I also used a lightning-fast announcer to shave off another .078 of a second.

We had three scripts, written to communicate the savings benefits of coordinated calling times, AT&T's program for reducing the long-distance charges for its Hispanic customers:

- In the first commercial, a young architect tries in vain to track down his flight attendant sweetheart. By using coordinated calling, they finally connect.

- In the second commercial, a family in the United States gathers together to call the grandparents back home to tell them that their grandson has a girlfriend.

- The third spot has a family calling a favorite uncle at work on a construction site at a prearranged time to wish him happy birthday. It featured a violin solo by the eight-year-old favorite nephew of the uncle.

I Can't Place the Accent

While auditioning actors for the commercials, we became so focused on creating the visually ideal Hispanic family that we neglected to consider that our actors all spoke a different Spanish—we had signed a Cuban mom, a Mexican dad, an Argentinean son, and a Guatemalan daughter. The talent had been signed, sealed, and delivered—approved up and down the AT&T chain of command. These actors were our "family." What to do? Perhaps proponents of mass marketing would say, "So what?" After all, mass marketers assume that, when blanketing everyone in a promotion campaign, you're bound to miss as many (if not more) than you hit. But in selective marketing, the point is to be *on* target, to really care about what your target audience cares about. That's the point of all the preparatory research. To ignore the facts, and in this case potentially offend various Hispanic groups, is tantamount to a marketing sin.

We did the only thing we could do: We spent more money to ensure that this campaign would make money for the client. We hired a second set of actors, but this group was chosen specifically for their accent, a "neutral" Columbian Spanish. They overdubbed the voices of the actors chosen for their "look."

NO MORE BUSY SIGNALS

The end result of this coordinated calling campaign was that more calls from AT&T customers in the States were being connected and not rebuffed by circuit busy signals. This shift in personal calling times had an important effect on business callers because it allowed their calls to get through during business hours. By utilizing selective marketing, AT&T was able to improve both service and revenue from the personal and business sectors of their long-distance business between the United States and Mexico.

Select Marketing Lessons

The AT&T campaign is an excellent example of the wide range of decision-making challenges selective marketing creative development may engender. This one had it all:

- A large select market that was really composed of several culturally diverse submarkets. We had to find the commonalities among the various Hispanic groups, while respecting their differences, all within the context of a select marketing program that would successfully reach them all.

- Social marketing issues. We had to figure out how to integrate an insular and foreign-speaking consumer group into a distinctly American company's services and change its calling habits to boot.

- Politics of big business. We had to find a way to work *around* the chaos of a changing marketplace (brought about in this case by deregulation) and *within* the tightening purse strings of the client caused by that internal upheaval.

In the face of all those elements, the vast and detailed knowledge base we had laid through the intensive research practices, which are always at the heart of any selective marketing program, gave us the flexibility and confidence needed to roll with the market punches. Throughout the AT&T experience, our firsthand perspective gave us an advantage over the competition.

13

LITE MAKES RIGHT:

Staying Abreast of Changing Tastes

for Kentucky Fried Chicken—KFC

- **Market:** White suburban baby boomers in the Northeast and urban African Americans.

- **Marketing Challenge:** Revitalize Kentucky Fried Chicken's slipping sales caused by the combination of an oversaturation in the fried chicken market, coupled with growing resistance to intake of fried foods in general.

- **Solution:** Test-market KFC's "lite" chicken to a double select market, both perceived as essential to the product.

- **Outcome:** Test-market results were spectacular.

The fried chicken category in the fast-turn world of quick-service restaurants (QSRs) had been experiencing a double-digit slide for the past three years, beginning in 1989. The downturn was attributed to a twofold cause: oversaturation of chicken-based outlets and the consumer shift away from high cholesterol and fried foods in general. The result was that Kentucky Fried Chicken was getting killed at the cash register.

KFC had decided to attack the problem at the menu level. It developed Lite 'n Crispy, a skinless fried chicken product that was to be positioned as a menu item that would win back the health-concerned suburban white baby boomers who had begun to pay more than lip service to the warnings from the medical community regarding the dangers of high-fat, high-cholesterol foods. After all, these boomers were approaching 50, and their mortality had moved from the sub- to the conscious part of their minds. KFC hoped that the Lite 'n Crispy product would save the day for the company. However, in preliminary testing, the product had not fared well.

So, before the plan to conduct full test-marketing for Lite 'n Crispy (intended for Atlanta and the Baltimore/Washington, D.C. area, preceding a rollout to the entire Northeast, and then nationwide) was carried out, the selective marketers at SMART were called in. Many millions were at stake. Chairman D. Wayne Calloway of KFC parent, Pepsico USA, stated that the launch of the Lite 'n Crispy product represented "the most important launch in the history of KFC."

TO MARKET, TO MARKET, TO SELL A THIN HEN

The decision to invest in segmented marketing instead of traditional mass marketing was made by KFC's Mike Kern, regional marketing manager, and SMART got the nod. Every advertising agency has its landmark campaign, and for SMART that campaign was the launch of KFC's Lite 'n Crispy Skinless Chicken.

Traditional mass-marketing product distribution cycles tend to flow the way the product category's promotional calendar flows. Generally, it can take from 18 months to three years to launch a national product rollout in the top 300 mass-media markets. In this case, however, the typical cycle in the chicken biz was necessarily truncated by the need to compete with powerful Roy Rogers and Church's campaigns then being run in targeted markets.

Using selective marketing strategies, SMART and Tracy-Locke (parent company Pepsico's ad agency) helped KFC make the adjustment to a quicker turnaround from concept to launch.

Working with the Tracy-Locke account team under vice president David Rogers, SMART began to immerse itself in KFC data—specifically, category statistical trends. Initially, we chose northeastern white baby boomers as the targeted consumers, because research showed they made up 32 percent of the population in an area that consumed 81 percent of the chicken in the QSR category. To reach them quickly, we earmarked local and spot media (as opposed to network buys), thereby telescoping long lead times into overnight electronic clearance and distribution and 48-hour program integration and broadcast.

Chicken Parts

While planning for the cut-through campaign that promised to give us a leg up on the competition in our target market—white baby boomers in the Northeast—we learned that Lite 'n Crispy had just failed miserably in a taste test with African Americans, who composed the highest indexing segment in the category (in fact, they dominated the chicken category in the Northeast and Midwest).

At that point, it was agreed that we would have to address *two* segmented markets simultaneously: white baby boomers in the Northeast and urban African Americans. And because of the time constraints, the client wanted this to be accomplished with a single campaign idea. This was a daunting challenge because the two markets had diametrically opposed attitudes toward KFC's lite chicken:

- As noted, white baby boomers were backing away from fried foods in general, hence the plan to give them lite—that is, skinless—fried chicken.

- African Americans rejected the lite product because for them the skin was a flavor enhancer.

Thus, our dilemma: how to address two market segments, one that regarded the skinless feature of the product as a benefit, the other that perceived it as a detriment?

In marketing, you have to develop almost a second sense for exactly what it is that makes your product, service, person, idea, or issue meaningful and relevant to your audience. This means you begin and end with intelligence gathering and consumer testing. The object of your research probes will be to find out exactly where to start building a case for the product or service with your audience—essentially, to find their buttons and learn which ones to push and which ones to leave alone.

We had already agreed that, in the boomer market, we were going to push the health button. We knew why these people were staying away from fried chicken. The African-American segment, however, proved more elusive to reach. And since data had shown that this market was traditionally a major component of KFC's heavy-user category, these consumers were not to be trifled with or offended. Furthermore, there was an urgency factor: SMART had two weeks to solve the problem.

New product introductions in the QSR category are handled with the precision of a military offensive maneuver. Franchisees are sold on the change. Food sources are established, restaurant crews are retrained, menus are revamped, cooking and preparations equipment is installed. And marketing programs are timed to build traffic the moment all is ready. The clock is constantly ticking for each of these elements and when one of them hits a snag it has to play catch-up. The research findings were a major snag that

> **SMART Marketing:**
>
> The deeper you probe market segments, the more likely you are to come up with usable similarities that allow you to combine segmentation efforts.

had to be addressed on the fly because the rest of the elements so critical to the launch could not be put on hold until we got the marketing problems solved.

TWO BIRDS WITH ONE STONE

Based upon meaningful insights and information provided by KFC field marketing people and franchisees that confirmed our research findings, we set about the task of developing a dual-edged strategy that would reach both our target markets. We decided to first go after African-American customers who still patronized KFC before going after the boomers we had already lost.

> **SMART Marketing:**
>
> The most significant difference between marketing a generic product to the masses and introducing a product that has been designed to fit the needs and desires of a targeted prospect is the money it takes to make an impression. It is far more efficient to sell a product to 200,000 people in one city than 200,000 people nationwide.

But before we could move forward, we had to confront what was, in a sense, a third market: KFC franchise owners, who had lost confidence in the company for two reasons. First, KFC did not have a sterling track record with new product development. For example, several attempts at introducing a barbecue sparerib product had misfired. Consequently, the franchisees were unhappy because the unchanging bill of fare was resulting in low consumer interest and, therefore, flagging sales. Second, the decision to change the company's name from Kentucky Fried Chicken to KFC (to eliminate the dreaded "F" word) had caused confusion in the market, which also resulted in less customer traffic. Furthermore, we were told that our campaign could in no way conflict with the national brand advertising created by Manny Gonzales's group on the East Coast at Young & Rubicam.

> **SMART Marketing:**
>
> The true challenge of selective marketing is adapting the product to the consumer, not the consumer to the product.

For many advertisers in the QSR category, one agency will handle the overall corporate image campaigns (Y&R in the case of KFC), another agency will handle the regional, company-owned stores (Tracy-Locke had the Northeast regional KFC outlets), and still another agency may be assigned to handle franchisee-owned restaurants on a city-by-city basis. Add to this mix agency assignments for the African-American consumer market, the Hispanic market, and the Asian market and you can have as many as five or six resources all developing marketing materials for a single advertiser. To avoid confusion, the lead agency (in this case, Y&R) generally sets the tone and the other agencies follow its direction. In this case, the regional agency, Tracy-Locke, utilizing selective marketing techniques, had come across a problem overlooked by the lead agency. Although we were charged with fixing the problem, it could not be done at the expense of the national brand advertising that was already running in the marketplace.

Taste Not, Want Not

Finally, we found ourselves at a disadvantage because we could not taste the product; it was testing on the East Coast, and we were in Los Angeles. Short of all of us going to Baltimore, there was no way to duplicate exactly what our target consumers were experiencing when they tried the product. (Having the chicken shipped and reheated was deemed not good enough, and it was determined that cooked-to-spec product could not accurately enough approximate in-store conditions.) Remember, the clock was ticking. It would be impossible for me to cross the country for a taste test and create the winning campaign at the same time. I would have to wing it.

Fortunately, our lack of firsthand product experience actually led us to the solution of how to promote the skinless product as both healthier than and as flavorful as the familiar fried chicken with skin. In lieu of tasting for relevant flavor analogies, we read the product preparation manuals. And that's where we found the answer.

Part of the preparation procedures for the Lite 'n Crispy product required marinating the chicken with "a combination of the Colonel's secret blend of herbs and spices to enhance the flavor while cooking." The marination process gave us the plausible and compelling reason why KFC's skinless chicken could be just as flavorful as its predecessors with skin.

Now all we had to do was find a way to convince KFC's African-American customer base that Lite 'n Crispy was so tasty, thanks to marination in the Colonel's secret recipe, that they wouldn't even miss the skin.

Even though the product met with resistance among our African-American taste-test respondents, there was no way the product could be reformulated. We reasoned that the taste-test failures were the result of unmet expectations on the part of our respondents. What they had been accustomed to was KFC fried chicken. What they received was KFC skinless chicken. If they compared the two, they were comparing apples to oranges. We had to position the taste characteristics of the Lite 'n Crispy product as a new experience, not an improvement on an old experience. After all, Lite 'n Crispy was a menu *extension* item, not a menu *replacement* item. This meant that we had to change their expectations *before* they tasted the product rather than alter their perceptions after tasting the product.

The marination angle also gave us a flavor enabler opportunity when addressing the primary target—suburban white baby boomers. Even though this market was key to KFC's growth in the category, it could not be won at the expense of KFC's core user group—urban African-American adults. The new campaign, therefore, had to influence these two equally important but vastly different target audiences. By leading with *flavor* as the primary benefit and *skinless* as a supporting benefit, we eliminated the "diet equals dull food" aspect of the product, which had proven a barrier to trial among African Americans in the test market.

TEMPTING THE MARKETS

SMART had the challenge of how to motivate a new segment of the market without alienating current customers. It had to be a creative platform that contained elements that both urban blacks and white suburban boomers could identify with as relevant and meaningful. In the case of KFC Lite 'n Crispy, we had to find a way to establish instant credibility by invoking something familiar and appealing to both target audiences. Once again, we relied on the universal language: music. Specifically, we chose the Temptations, a group that had proven itself over the decades as cross-generational, cross-cultural, and—more important to KFC—cross-market. The Temptations would appeal to white suburban baby boomers and urban blacks because their music had had a profound effect upon the cultural coming of age of both of the targeted selective markets. In addition, the group's recent 1991 double-platinum hit with Rod Stewart, a platinum Christmas album, and their sold-out shows with the Four Tops had brought them back into the limelight. Another publicity bonus was that the McCaulay Culkin movie, *My Girl,* was in the works, which had the public once again humming the Temptations hit that was the namesake of the movie.

> **SMART Marketing:**
>
> The use of common denominators between diverse market segments permits economies of scale to allow increased creative latitude.

At SMART, we keep our segment channels open with research probes, attitude surveys, social gatherings, benefit attendance, and public-service support. I had designed the Temptations' album covers in the late 1960s, so I still had my Motown contacts and knew the Temptations were currently in the studio recording. In short, SMART was plugged in, which enabled us to deliver on a drop-dead timeline.

Within the two-week deadline, SMART presented the Temptations–KFC Lite 'n Crispy "Flavor's More Than Skin Deep" campaign. The deal we negotiated called for the Temptations to produce the KFC radio commercials to coincide with their current Motown Records recording dates. Then we worked out the details of a national rollout in record time.

TOO GOOD TO BE TRUE

As the old saying goes, "The operation was a success, but the patient died." Ironically, the Temptations singing "Flavor's more than skin deep" for KFC was a hit with one customer too many. The Food and Drug Administration's David Kessler (rumored to be an avid Motown fan) had heard the ad (remember, the D.C. area was one of our test markets), and it started him thinking about the "truth in advertising" of a product billed both as "lite" and "fried." He decided it was a no-go and put the kibosh on Lite 'n Crispy.

Footnote: Fortunately, for SMART, it was not the end of a beautiful concept. Mike Kern at KFC was so pleased with the performance of SMART on the KFC Lite 'n Crispy launch that he requested we be set loose on capturing the African-American market. He gave us a KFC pilot store in Baltimore to completely reengineer from menu to store design. To make a long story short, within 90 days, that store had lines around the block. SMART had helped bring about one of the biggest turnarounds in KFC history—another testimony to the value of selective marketing techniques.

Select Marketing Lessons

All successful selective marketing efforts begin and end with a question. The first question is always: "What can we do?" The last question is always: "How did we do?" In between the first and the last questions, SMART learns how to adapt its clients' products or services to the most likely prospect by becoming more meaningful and more relevant to the needs and desires of the selected prospect. The key to reaching out to those segments of the population that have an unmet need or desire for your client's product is a well-tested network of segment information channels.

Once you're plugged in, the intelligence gathering begins. The primary objective in the KFC Lite 'n Crispy launch was to motivate a new segment of the market without alienating current customers. To do that effectively, we had to shift the focus of the advertising from the product attributes that we knew were problematic to the product's primary benefit: flavor that was "more than skin deep." Coupled with identifying the right celebrity endorser for our double target market, we were able to deliver the necessary credibility to two market segments with very different takes on the product.

The Temptations disarmed customer resistance in the first eight bars of "Flavor's More Than Skin Deep." Thus charmed, our primary prospects were romanced into trying the new product. Blacks didn't think of it as a boomer-oriented campaign and boomers didn't think of it as a black-oriented campaign. Both consumer groups did exactly what SMART believed they would: yield to their own Temptations.

14

TAKING STOCK:

Ensuring the Future of an Automotive Giant

for Ford Motor Company

- **Selected Markets:** Wall Street, Washington, D.C., and Ford Motor Company Shareholders, Customers, and Employees.

- **Marketing Challenge:** Assure these various segments of the public that in spite of what appear to be significant losses—Ford was losing millions of dollars each week—Ford Motor Company has invested $3 billion to keep its future bright.

- **Marketing Solution:** Expose each of the target audiences to Ford Motor Company's worldwide areas of success that ensure the future growth of the company.

- **Outcome:** Ford stock rallied from 16⅞ in 1981 to $80 a share in 1987 and the company set the agenda that led to the rebirth of quality within the domestic automotive industry. By 1989, after two years of record profits, Ford made more money than its much bigger rival, General Motors.

Through two world wars, Ford Motor Company grew into a multinational monolith with far-flung interests around the globe. But if ever the excesses and value judgments associated with mass-market thinking in the 1950s, 1960s, and 1970s were to be assigned a prototype, Detroit's Big Three auto manufacturers—Ford, Chrysler, and General Motors—would be it. During the three decades following World War II, each of them made marketing decisions based on what the other two were doing, instead of staying in touch with the changing wants and needs of their customers. And while they were busy watching each other, foreign competition was charting the growing dissatisfaction in the marketplace.

OUTSIDE INTERESTS

For 20 years, Datsun had been watching with greedy interest the increasing disenchantment of the American consumer for the Big Three's "planned obsolescence" practices. During that time, Japanese engineers had come to the United States, photographed our country roads and city streets, moved in with American families disguised as exchange students, recorded our habits and practices in detail, and reported to Japan with mind-numbing precision all they had learned. Within a few years, this wealth of market research and the implementation of statistical quality control procedures, as defined by Marshall Plan quality control guru W. Edwards Deming, paid off: The imports began to roll onto American soil. Soon, imports outnumbered domestic automobiles in six western states, and in the Northeast, Audi, Volvo, BMW, and Mercedes began to make inroads against American auto manufacturers.

Still, it took the failure and subsequent bailout of Chrysler Corporation before senior management in Detroit began to stand up and take notice. But by this time, domestic manufacturers were faced with car lots full of unsold inventory, and many dealer organizations had begun to hedge their bets by branching into foreign car distribution agreements. By the 1980s, the Big Three were losing millions of dollars in sales every day, and Wall Street was more than a little alarmed.

MULTIPLE PERSONALITY

The Ford Motor Company was not going to roll over and play dead. In the early 1980s, when this crisis erupted, I was brought in by Charlie Moss, head of the creative department at Wells, Rich, Green, the corporate advertising agency for the Ford Motor Company. My task was to convey Ford's image to the many segments of its public through the use of selective marketing.

Under the direction of Ford CEO Phillip Caldwell, the company had a solid grasp on its situation. It was losing market share. Its products were not up to snuff. It had low morale. Ford stock was going down. The company had the imports biting at its toes. It was time to do something. Ford management had been aware of the problem for several years. They knew this was a trend and not just a hiccup in the research, and they were determined to accomplish two sets of goals:

1a. Stop the erosion of brand share.

b. Set the agenda for the future of the American automotive industry.

c. Establish among Wall Street, Washington, D.C., (as a major customer of Detroit and with the power to regulate foreign auto imports) and shareholders, customers, and employees that Ford had the staying power, the resources, the technology, and, most of all, the love of the car business to succeed now and well into the future.

   d. Buy enough time to translate the company's verbal commitment to quality into products that could reignite America's confidence in Ford products.

2a. Let people know Ford was in tune with the times.

   b. Acknowledge consumer concerns about quality and reliability by making significant improvements in every Ford product.

   c. Be 12 to 13 months ahead of the marketplace in bringing innovation to the consumer.

   d. Commit $3 billion to build the dramatically styled Taurus and Sable to create excitement in the North American automotive operating division.

This effort evolved into three distinct campaigns that spanned almost a decade. Because of the long lead times (three to four years) associated with automotive manufacturing changeovers, our corporate marketing efforts had to accommodate the promise, the realization, and the results of Ford Motor Company's multibillion-dollar investment. The first of these campaigns was "The Incredible World of Ford," which Wells referred to as "the factory tour." This campaign dealt with "the promise." Jim Lawrence, then executive vice president at Wells, Rich, Green, recalls that everything was a bit depressed in Detroit at that time (1982) and the goal of this first phase of corporate advertising was to publicly set the agenda for the company. There was a hell of a lot going on at Ford back then, but obviously it would take quite some time to bring this new generation of products to market. Therefore, our new corporate campaign for Ford Motor Company incorporated three separate and distinct phases:

- *The Promise:* "The Incredible World of Ford," which gave a broad overview of the company's commitment to the global economy.

- *The Realization:* "There's a Ford in America's Future," which portrayed the broad expanse of Ford Motor Company's worldwide successes.

- *The Results:* "Quality Is Job 1," which delineated the commitment to quality as expressed by the employees of Ford's automotive divisions.

THE PROMISE

"If you could see tomorrow, the way it looks to us today, you'd say, 'incredible!' " With these lyrics, Wells, Rich, Green introduced America to the promise of an engineering revolution quietly taking place from top to bottom of the world's second largest automotive manufacturer. The message contained in "The Incredible World of Ford" campaign was so powerful and so compelling that the agency found itself having to pull the campaign after just one month due to the overwhelming interest from the public to actually take Ford Motor Company up on its offer to "come tour our factory and see for yourself."

Jim Lawrence believes that there has always been a great credibility to what Ford has said. "Sometimes this has worked better than others, but if this belief had not been there, this and subsequent campaigns would not have met with such unqualified acceptance and success," he reflects. America wanted to believe in its automobiles and Ford Motor Company was about to give Americans something concrete to believe in: quality. People loved and hated Ford. "A lot of people love Ford. I don't know if that is necessarily true of Chrysler or General Motors," comments Jim

Lawrence, summing up the inherent goodwill that greeted Ford Motor Company's corporate advertising efforts at the dawn of the 1980s.

Initially, the failures of the domestic automotive industry led us to recommend that the segments of the public Ford had to address first—that is, our selected markets—were those very close to home: Wall Street, Washington, Ford stockholders, consumers, and employees, and, most important, the other members of the Big Three. In fact, special attention was paid to Detroit media outlets to send, in Jim's words, "a memo across the street." We were clearly setting an agenda for Detroit with each phase of Ford's corporate advertising effort. And by no means was Ford doing this in the dark. The company set its priorities, doing mountains of research in the form of consumer tracking surveys that delineated how the public perceived Ford vis-à-vis the automotive industry, both domestic and imported. The company was determined to get the facts straight before setting its course of action. Once it did this, the company knew exactly what to promise its selected markets.

In spite of the general feeling that Detroit had lost touch with its marketplace, this was not the case at Ford Motor Company. There the issue became not just identifying the situation, but acting to correct it. Ford's management knew the company had been great once. They also knew that the company's market share was eroding. The key issues to Ford's management were where they were going to go, how they were going to get there, what it was going to cost, how they were going to measure the results, and, most important, what they were going to be known for when they finally got there.

A Partnership with Labor

As the 1970s wound down, there was a lot of gloom and doom among those who worked in the domestic automobile business.

Times were rough. Ford Motor Company had to start in its own backyard.

A key element in Ford's strategy was to bring excitement back to the people who designed and built its automobiles. It was critical to get Ford employees enthusiastic again about where the company was headed. Walls had to come down. Walls between management and labor. Walls between supervisors and line workers. Walls between those who designed and engineered Fords, Lincolns, and Mercurys and those who built them on the vast assembly lines all across the country. One of the first things to go was the separate parking lots for managers and assembly line workers. Quality circles were organized so that, instead of decisions being made from the top down, they could be arrived at from the bottom up by those actually held responsible for building each and every automobile.

Zero-defects programs and statistical quality control procedures began to make a world of difference in the "things gone wrong" surveys used to determine customer satisfaction levels with each of the domestic and imported auto nameplates sold in America. By starting with its own employees, Ford intended to bring pride of workmanship back to Detroit.

Taking Stock of the Stock

Ford stock was not doing well at all in the early 1980s. It was down—way down. The analysts on Wall Street were not paying attention to what was happening in the assembly plants in Dearborn and Cleveland. They were distracted by what they were reading in the papers and hearing on the evening news. Horror stories of Ford losing $1 million a day made far better copy than the advancements being made by other Ford divisions such as Ford Aerospace, Ford Glass, Ford Electronics, and Ford Credit. These, of course, were major profit centers in their own right, but nobody knew it. Wall Street equated Ford Motor Company with its domestic automotive business and little else.

Image erosion regarding the products of Detroit was in full swing from the late 1970s on. "Don't buy a domestic car built on Mondays or Fridays because the workers are drunk or hung over" was a mantra spread by such popular best-sellers as *On a Clear Day You Can See General Motors* and *Japan in the Passing Lane.* Both small and large investors were becoming increasingly alarmed by what they were hearing and reading about the slump in domestic auto sales and the growing popularity of imports. So were those to whom these investors turned for advice.

Outside Influences

Ford Motor Company chairman Philip Caldwell and his international management team realized early on that, as important as the individual and institutional investor were, they typically either relied on or were influenced by the opinions of others. Specifically, in the case of Ford stock, they were being influenced by brokers, fund managers, stock analysts, or financial advisors who generally had little or no idea of the scope of Ford's worldwide operations. Wells realized that to influence shareholders or potential shareholders, we had to clearly communicate Ford's wide assortment of global success stories to their financial advisors; hence, shareholders became our secondary selected market, and their advisors became our primary selected market.

This made our job more difficult, because this target audience was considerably more hype-proof than the average institutional or individual investor. Financial advisors listened to the industry analysts at the brokerage houses. These were their experts. Industry analysts make their living by separating a company's investor relations department "propaganda" from the cold, hard facts of the company's performance in

> **SMART Marketing:**
>
> To reach members of a select market, it may sometimes be necessary to go through their advisors, or "key influencers," who then become the primary select market.

the marketplace. Furthermore, these advisors once drove Fords, Lincolns, and Mercurys themselves—that is, before they traded up to Mercedes-Benzes and BMWs. These securities advisors were the first people called by individual investors when they were trying to decide whether to hold or fold their positions in Ford shares. These advisors were also the ones with the most to lose if an investment in Ford proved to be imprudent. If they no longer believed in the product, how confident would they be recommending the stock? The time had come for us to set the record straight.

THE REALIZATION

At the same time that the Ford team at Wells was busy getting a fix on our next target audience and figuring out how to best approach them, we also had to learn more about our client in order to, as Jim Lawrence put it, ". . . let Wall Street and the present and prospective Ford shareholder know that there was a whole other world going on out here." In other words, the theme of the next campaign was to say, in lay terms, "Hey, this ain't Chrysler, baby." That is to say that we had to communicate clearly and dramatically that Ford Motor Company was, is, and will always be a global powerhouse. In other words, we had to tell our selected markets, "There's a Ford in America's Future."

SMART Marketing:

To stay connected with any market, no matter how select, it sometimes helps to think of the people who make up that market as a single, composite individual, then determine the real-life experiences and prejudices that your message will have to overcome.

Ford engineers had designed the Escort, the first "world car" to come out of the Big Three, which encompassed so-called European styling and quality control in the international marketplace. That effort, along with zero-defects manufacturing initiatives at the engine, power-train, and assembly facilities were the silver lining in the storm clouds raining down Ford's seven-digit daily losses. Quality cost money and we had to position these expenditures as the price of progress, not the evidence of failure in the domestic marketplace.

In 1983, the Ford Escort became the best-selling car in Europe and received the Car of the Year award, ironically, in Japan. Riding on that success, the following year, Ford introduced its "European concept" car, the Taurus, to the American public. Both the Escort and the Taurus were "overnight" success stories that had taken a decade of planning and preparation.

In addition to all that was new and exciting around the world, business for several of Ford Motor Company's domestic operations—Ford Aerospace, Ford Trucks, and Ford Tractors—was booming. Nevertheless, to Wall Street, Ford spelled automotive, and automotive stocks were dogs that would not hunt. It was the job of Wells, Rich, Green to change that perception. Bob Kaplan and I were brought in at this stage to do exactly that.

Under the direction of Wells executive vice presidents Jim Lawrence, Paul Margulies, and Bob Wilvers, we attacked this seemingly impossible task. The first step was to identify the various success stories that could be used to, as a popular song of the day proclaimed, "Turn The Beat Around."

Under the Hood

The Ford Motor Company is like a nation unto itself; the shear scope of its worldwide operations is daunting. Our team began the laborious task of drilling down and labeling each and every level of contact that impacted a single decision by private and institutional investors to buy or sell Ford stock, to buy or not buy Ford cars, and to buy or reject Ford's vision for the future. Our mission was to create a corporate advertising program geared to influence each of those levels. We had to make our selected audiences see Ford's titanic losses as something other than an approaching iceberg. We had to turn what was perceived as multi-million-dollar losses into what they really were—multi-million-dollar new product investments by a company with pockets deep enough to sustain such an investment and much, much more.

Part of this objective was to find the right phrase that would say it all and that we could use in our promotional materials. We had to make it clear that Ford's future was bright, that rumors of its demise were exaggerated. Margulies and Wilvers dug into

> **SMART Marketing:**
>
> The difference between opinion and knowledge can mean the difference between the success and failure of a company.

Ford's past to find its promise for the future, and they found it in a line credited to Henry Ford himself:

There's a Ford in America's Future.

As mentioned earlier, this phase of the Ford corporate campaign was to make sure our selected markets knew that Ford was a whole lot more than just its consumer automotive division: that one of every three trucks on the road was a Ford; that Ford tractors were the best-selling tractors in the world; that the majority of satellites that circle the globe were put there by Ford Aerospace; that the same computers that fly the Boeing 747 guide the Lincoln Continental; that the best-selling car in the world (the Escort) was a Ford; that the winner of the German Auto Show was a Ford; and even that the Car of the Year in Japan was a Ford. To do that, Wells placed double-page spreads in the *Wall Street Journal,* the *New York Times,* the *Washington Post,* the *Detroit Free Press,* the *Chicago Tribune,* the *Los Angeles Times,* and dozens of other dailies, as well as in *Time* and *Newsweek.* We left no media stone unturned.

Chase Scene

While the media blitz was doing its job of reeducating Wall Street about Ford's ongoing divisional successes, the automotive giant's

Special Vehicle Operations Group was poised and ready to captivate investors' imaginations with the rebirth of the "muscle car," in the form of the high-performance SVO Mustang. The SVO had been designed to compete in the sports car arena, where sales were being captured and held by the foreign makes—Porsches, Lamborghinis, Ferraris, and Ford's eternal nemesis, the Chevrolet Corvette. Wells was assigned the task of promoting the SVO Mustang, but it was a balancing act, for we had been directed to stress performance over muscle.

Ralph Nader's best-seller, *Unsafe at Any Speed,* had tolled the death knell not only for the rear-engined Chevy Corvair but also for the street-ready, super-stock performance cars of the early 1960s. In 1961 it was possible to buy a screaming 425-horsepower, 409-cubic-inch, four-speed Chevy SuperSport, Ford Mustang, Pontiac GTO, or Dodge Charger and do 0 to 60 miles per hour in little more than a heartbeat. Street-racing fatalities and emission control systems led to the formal withdrawal of factory-sponsored high-performance competition and the manufacturing of muscle cars. The subsequent gas crisis and lowered speed limits (to 55 miles per hour) put the last nails in that coffin.

However, by the early 1980s, Ford and General Motors were again looking at performance as a marketing tool to use against the onslaught of the imports that were bound by no such restrictions and were beginning to make real strides in the high-performance arena. But even as late as 1984, Ford's legal department forbade us from touting 0- to-60-mile-per-hour speeds in our advertising because they felt it would be an endorsement by Ford of violating the national speed code, which the company had no intention of doing.

SMART Marketing:

A selected market sometimes can be further divided into even more select "submarkets."

Fortunately, the SVO Mustang was given a head start when the California Highway Patrol (CHP) came looking for the car that would enable its officers to keep up with and catch the new menace on the freeways of southern California: the very high-performance sports cars that were the Mustang's foreign-built competitors. As soon as the CHP chose Ford's SVO Mustang, Bob Kaplan and I lost no time in taking advantage of the situation. After stalling a few times, we hit one out of the park with

This Ford Chases Porsches for a Living.

Not only had we scripted a memorable headline, we had found another excellent selected market segment to tap: law enforcement publications. Within a few months, 22 law enforcement agencies added fleets of SVO Mustangs to their pursuit rosters. I have also wondered if this particular ad encouraged government institutional investors to hold their funds' positions (totaling millions of shares) in Ford Motor Company.

Thinking Globally Causes a Reaction Locally

One of the very first spreads of the "There's a Ford in America's Future" phase of the corporate campaign showed a gigantic Ford logo rising out of the sea, with the headline, "We're Big over There." From this point on, the campaign was a success. The ad that proclaimed "One Out of Every Three Trucks on the Road Is a Ford" won the agency a letter of praise from the head of Ford's Truck Division for ending the doom-and-gloom attitude that was spilling over into his highly successful operation. An ad that portrayed a Ford Ranger crossing the finish line in the Baja 1000 race in Mexico ("Toyota and Datsun Are Two Hours behind This Picture") was one of the first to foretell that the second car in America's garages would soon be a truck. But the most important results of this phase of the campaign according to Wells, Rich, Greene and the management at Ford were "optimism and a positive mind-set toward the future and Ford Motor Company's role in it." In addition to print, there were also television executions touting Ford Motor Company's success in Europe and in aerospace, which ran in the influential markets of New York, Washington, D.C., Detroit, Chicago, and Los Angeles. Within two short years the "Ford in America's Future" phase of the campaign had set the stage for the natural evolution to the final phase of the campaign.

The commitment to quality had by this time (1984–1985) filtered down to every facet of Ford's business, from the men and women on the line to the dealers and service technicians in the field and their quality care programs. One of the things that corporate advertising should do is set the blueprint and establish the agenda in the marketplace so that the company is as well-postured as it can be in both good times and bad. In the case of Ford Motor Company, we relied upon universal themes to reach our selected markets. A U.S. senator felt as good about the best-selling car in the world being a Ford Escort as did a Wall Street investment banker. A service technician in Chicago was as impressed that one out of every three trucks on the road was a Ford as was the riveter on the assembly line at Ford's Nashville truck plant. Of course, if you were in the market for a new car it didn't hurt to know that a Ford had been voted Car of the Year in Japan or that it had won honors at the German Auto Show.

THE RESULTS

The third tier of the Ford Motor Company corporate campaign was ready when the product improvement promises became improved product realities. The first new small cars introduced by Ford in 1981, the Escort went on to become the best-selling car in the world. It was then that Ford began stressing employee involvement in the quality process. Once this took effect, Ford began to turn the corner. Both attendance and morale picked up once Ford employees realized that the management of the company was serious about the commitment to build better vehicles. By 1984, the Aero cars, Thunderbird, Cougar, Mark VII, and Tempo/Topaz had caught on with the American public.

Between 1981 and 1995, in conjunction with these three awareness campaigns ("The Incredible World of Ford", "There's a Ford in America's Future," and "Quality Is Job 1") directed at Wall Street, Washington, and Ford shareholders, customers, and employees, several important goals were achieved:

- On Wall Street, Ford stock began to go up and eventually rallied from $60 a share in 1985 to $80 a share in 1987.

- Quality did improve. In 1981, at the launch of "The Incredible World of Ford" phase of the campaign, Ford had been 15 points below General Motors on a key quality tracking survey. Twelve years later, in 1993, Ford was rated 12 points above GM, a net gain of 27 points.

- Three years after the campaign was initiated, Ford went from six-digit-a-day losses to a $2.9 billion profit and a car and truck market share increase of 21.7 percent.

- In 1985, Ford reported the highest net income in the company's history.

- By 1990, Ford had five of the ten best-selling vehicles in America. Ford's share of the car market was 22 percent and trucks were at 29.9 percent, the highest in the past decade.

Select Marketing Lessons

Two very important selective marketing lessons were revealed in the Ford corporate campaign:

1. Look beyond the obvious when identifying a select market. You may have to divide your audience into primary and secondary segments. In the case of Ford, if we had directed our campaign at consumers and not at those people who influenced and motivated the consumers' perceptions of Ford products (reflected in the joke that *Ford* is an acronym for "found on road dead" or "fix or repair daily"), we would have failed in our efforts to reestablish Ford as a company whose stock and products were safe investments.

2. Stay on the alert throughout any select marketing campaign for the opportunity to extend the reach to include other circumstantial select consumers. Select marketing techniques are not synonymous with narrow marketing techniques. In the Ford campaign, because we jumped on the opportunity presented by another select market—the California Highway Patrol—we were able to simultaneously present the new image of Ford's automotive division and convince investors of the viability of Ford stock—and sell a lot of police cars.

15

GETTING A WEB SITE ON THE RIGHT TRACK:

Training an Enthusiastic Select Market

for Athearn Trains in Miniature

- **Market:** Current and prospective model railroad enthusiasts worldwide.

- **Marketing Challenge:** Capture the attention of leading-edge enthusiasts and keep them coming back for more.

- **Marketing Solution:** Develop a Web domain that has the same appeal as the subjects the selected market is drawn to recreate in miniature.

- **Outcome:** We were able to build upon the interest and excitement generated by the client's product line to entertain model railroad enthusiasts with technology, interactivity, and a steady flow of meaningful information with which to make their purchase decisions.

The Internet is a selective marketer's dream come true. Potentially, 55 million early adapters worldwide can now type your product category into their random search engines. If your Web site comes up in their search, your prime prospects can pump out reams of information on your product or service. That's the way the World Wide Web is supposed to work.

Unfortunately, it is more like the World Wide Wait. The Internet has not yet lived up to the hype, but increased bandwidth is promised "any decade now," and streaming audio and video holds great promise. Speed is indeed a problem for the instant-gratification crowd that such hype attracts in droves. However, this leaves millions and millions of on-line viewers, surfers, lurkers, browsers, and buyers who are willing to wait until the graphics download, some Java Applet remembers their password, their computer reboots, or their netlink is successful. Those actively seeking information (rather than entertainment) will generally wait. People who are willing to wait for stuff that keenly interests them are called *enthusiasts*.

Generally, enthusiasts are highly motivated buyers. Addicts to their passion for . . . whatever. Our client, Athearn Trains in Miniature, loves enthusiasts. The challenge for SMART was not to help Athearn define its selected market, but rather to help the company expand its business by making those who were nonenthusiasts more enthusiastic about model railroading.

TO THE ENTHUSIAST, SEGMENT INFORMATION *IS* ENTERTAINMENT

Athearn connects its massive collection of over 1,800 HO-scale cars and locomotives to its selected market through traditional hobby publications such as *Model Railroader* and *Railroad Model Craftsman*. SMART research discovered that the average reader will interact with *Model Railroader* magazine 15 to 20 times during a month. Readers keep issues accessible year after year. Model railroad enthusiasts and their first cousins, rail fans, are as serious about their chosen pastime as are golfers, boating enthusiasts, or Chicago Cubs fans. Research told us early on that information is the only reason our selected audience reads the ads in the hobby magazines.

Members of our selected market already knew all they needed to know about Athearn from the hobby magazines. Athearn's new owners were not looking to make waves—just improvements in the company's financial and manufacturing performance. They were astute enough to realize that their market was watching every move they made because their customers were concerned that the new ownership would change a brand they had come to count on for low prices and high quality. The SMART strategy was to give those watchers something to talk about. The new team at Athearn had developed an ambitious calendar of new product releases. SMART had the job of getting the word out.

A Defining Moment

Irv Athearn did not start his model train company back in 1948 simply to get rich. He loved trains. Traditionally, companies that service the thousands of enthusiast market segments tend to be founded by enthusiasts, grown by astute managers, and acquired by watchful conglomerates. The key to success with any demanding customers is understanding what drives their need to purchase and then catering to it. This is certainly not brain surgery, but it is a point that can get lost in the transition from enthusiast founder to enthusiastic manager to optimistic investor.

Would the new owners change Irv Athearn's formula for success, or would they build on it? Well, Mike Geddes, the new chairman and Bob Macias, the president and the manufacturing genius behind the majority of products in the vast Athearn line, are not into change for the sake of change. In fact, they questioned the need for any marketing at all. Business was booming as well-healed baby boomers rediscovered their love of toy trains and indulged themselves.

First, SMART talked to the trade—an easy task because most of the country's hobby shops are listed in the back of *Model Railroader* magazine and thus were easy to find. These are folks who love to talk, especially about trains. We found that the retail trade basically consists of hobby enthusiasts who found a way to make money on their interest and knowledge. The trade told us that, although Athearn was great, "they were leaving a lot of money on the table," meaning that smaller companies were eating into Athearn's share of the market. Hobbyists complained that items went out of stock and were unavailable for months and sometimes years. Like most non-consumer-oriented companies, Athearn believed its customer to be the distributor, not the end user. This is the deadliest trap in selective marketing.

Here was a 50-year-old company that had practically built the universally popular hobby of model railroading, yet, in terms of marketing, it was still in its infancy. We proposed that Athearn start acting like the industry leader it was. Model railroading is a creative endeavor, so to lead the pack, Athearn had to be more creative than anybody else in the field. Our research told us that people who spend vast amounts of time and money on escapist hobbies are not particularly interested in reality. They live in a fantasy world and Athearn's products (or anybody else's, for that matter) are fine until they interrupt the fantasy by failing to function as expected. We had to position Athearn as more than a big company that sells a lot of HO-scale trains. We had to appeal to our selected market's fantasy or interior life. Our strategy was to convince the model railroad enthusiast that, because of the immense number of Athearn cars and locomotives in use on model railroads across the nation, Athearn is, in fact, *The Biggest Little Railroad in America.*

However, to truly dimensionalize a manufacturing company located in Compton, California, as the Biggest Little Railroad in America, we needed something that went beyond the limitations of the flat, four-color, monthly magazine page. We needed something more dramatic, more dynamic, more interactive. The Biggest Little Railroad in America needed to be brought to life. Our answer was www.athearn.com.

START SMALL AND GROW,
START BIG AND DIE, BUT START

Nothing begets endless pontification like the decision to launch a company Web site. Leo Burnett USA does it best—one page; the company name, address, phone number, and rotating logo. Period. Leo Burnett USA observed rule number one: If you intend to have a Web address, get it registered, get it up on a server, get it functional and correct. Then start your internal debates. A Web site is not an ad or a TV spot. It is a continuing work in progress.

> **SMART Marketing:**
>
> Always look beyond traditional advertising vehicles to expand your brand's exposure to your selected market. Nothing is as powerful as a surprise encounter to reinforce awareness among your targets.

Consider the situation at Athearn, a traditional manufacturing-to-distributor sales organization with highly developed promotional channels. New management brings new thinking. Tim Geddes, the new vice president of sales and marketing at Athearn, wanted to expand Athearn's sphere of influence. Almost everybody recognizes the Lionel name, but few outside of the 500,000 or so domestic model railroad enthusiasts know of Athearn. Tim believed that Athearn could expand its business only by expanding the hobby. The Internet provided a global market of 55 million or so active participants, predominantly male, technically savvy early adapters. The average age of these Netizens skewed younger than that of Athearn's selected baby boomer, so there was potential for market longevity to boot. Add to that the fact that the Web already hosts a substantial international community of rail and model rail user groups, bulletin boards, chat rooms and Web sites, and you have a no-lose situation. Or so we all thought.

For the Love of It
Enthusiast market segments are among the most difficult selective markets to persuade because of their significant knowledge of

their specific area of interest. Generally, they cannot be hyped. This is because enthusiasts find some degree of joy in talking, debating, researching, debunking, verifying, testing, and endorsing every conceivable aspect of their hobby. Perhaps no hobby contains more experts on minutiae than those who love, follow, photograph, ride, and model America's railroads. "Rivet counters," "foamers," "railheads"—the sobriquets are endless. And with the advent of the Internet, this diverse legion of enthusiasts has found the perfect medium for self-expression and interaction.

It's Not Politically Correct If It's Not Prototypically Correct

The Internet is also the great equalizer. *Handles,* or pseudonyms for anonymous visitors to the various rail-oriented sites, are another way of stripping off the age, race, gender, and cultural differences among enthusiasts and allowing them to lead with their knowledge of the subject at hand. Such anonymity also allows marketers the ability to pose as enthusiasts. This dynamic offered Athearn a dimension in building its Web site that eluded the company in building its products: immediate feedback. And that's what we got, every step of the way.

SMART Marketing:

When focusing on a select audience, don't miss any opportunity to go "undercover" as a member of your target market for immediate feedback.

Rail-oriented chat rooms on CompuServe and America Online held ongoing critiques about everything from the quality of our HTML code to the download time of our Web site graphics. Soon, like everything else connected with model railroading, experts began to appear in the various chat rooms on—you guessed it—the Athearn Web site.

The Athearn account team at SMART would lurk in these chat rooms, as would Athearn managers, just to see the response to the latest changes to the Web site. The SMART team also made suggestions as though they were coming from enthusiasts ("What they should be doing is this . . ."), to test consumer response for new additions to the Athearn Web site before they were launched.

Lights, Camera, Reaction

One of the areas we pretested for the Athearn Web site was the development of an ongoing, on-line, railroad-oriented soap opera. America's railroads have long been a favorite subject of the pulp fiction genre. In the 1930s and 1940s, railroad potboilers were a staple of the dime-store novel. The concept fit in nicely with our positioning of Athearn as the Biggest Little Railroad in America.

SMART created the episodic adventure, *Empire,* which told the story of a small midwestern railroad, the Athearn, Atlantic & Pacific, that was caught in the middle of a tug-of-war between two rail giants, Eastrail and Westrail, both striving to be the first transcontinental rail network in the nation. We wrote the historical backstory and the first installment and gave readers five alternate endings to choose from. By tallying the responses, we could then let the story proceed based upon the collective vision of the readers.

Of course, throughout this great rail saga, any time we mentioned a freight car, passenger car, or locomotive, we offered a hyperlink to the Athearn on-line catalog so the reader could see a picture of the Athearn model and a background blurb about the prototype.

YOU CAN'T LAY RAILS WITHOUT NAILS

When you get your first train set, it usually comes with a circle of sectional track. After a while, you long for something more permanent. You pull the track up off the floor, put it on a sheet of plywood, and add to it with more realistic flex-track. As the years go by and you become a more accomplished model railroad enthusiast, the flex-track just doesn't look right, so you tear it up and lay down individual wooden cross ties and code-70 rail affixed with rail spikes and precisely aligned with a track gauge. Each enthusiast has his or her rite of passage. So it is with the Athearn Web site.

We started with a basic Web marketing platform. Central to that platform was the commitment to provide a customer service utilizing HTML technology that was cost-prohibitive by any other means. The first leg of that service was to provide our selected market with a complete reference guide to every one of the more than 1,800 items offered by Athearn. This on-line guide would provide the model railroad enthusiast with color pictures, prices, part numbers, assembly instructions, mechanical specs, and item numbers for everything the company made. The second leg of that service was to enhance our selected market's enjoyment of the hobby by providing information, entertainment, and shared experiences directly related to prototype and model railroading. SMART saw to it that Athearn observed the first rule of Internet Marketing: Get on-line first and work out content later. It made all the difference in the world.

Avoid Technology for Technology's Sake

Although I strongly recommend taking a long, hard look at new media before committing significant dollars, I do avocate getting in early to get your feet wet. One of the great benefits of this strategy is that you can make all your mistakes early on, before too many people notice. We specifically resisted the newest technology in building the Athearn Web site because we knew going in that the more esoteric the Web application, the more limited the potential audience. We utilized an interesting method to test wide receptivity before launching the site. First we nested a mock Athearn Web site on our own www.smartcomm.com. Then we leaked word of the preview site in two or three of the model rail–oriented chat rooms. Bingo. Within a few days of eavesdropping in these same chat rooms, we knew which graphic techniques (such as animation) did not play on AOL, which pages were coming out like mud on low-resolution black-and-white monitors, and which areas of the site were getting the most traffic. We have utilized this technique to test several Web site projects since then, all with insightful results.

SMART Web and interface designers launched the actual first-stage version of the Athearn Web site minus the elaborate animated splash page, with a core page containing both graphic and text interface links, and with downloadable product schematics all based upon feedback gained from the nested Athearn site comments. As members of our selected market made comments and suggestions about our episodic rail adventure, *Empire,* we compiled their e-mail addresses in a database to be used for future online promotional events. Frequent updates ensured repeat traffic and helped promote word of mouth. A new products section allowed us to provide our selected market with advanced notice to of things to come. But most important of all, the Athearn Web site provided our client with a means of constant dialogue and feedback with an audience hungry for the latest news from the Biggest Little Railroad in America.

Select Marketing Lessons

SMART's experience with Athearn yielded several valuable selective marketing lessons:

- The more enthusiastic your audience is, the more critical they are of your product or service. You have to examine your marketing from the enthusiast's point of view.

- It is important to approach such consumers respectfully, because they are constantly communicating among themselves and have a great deal of influence on each other's buying perceptions.

- When trying to build a link between your product and your customer, it is essential to bring them together in an atmosphere of informative support. The Internet provides the perfect forum to do just that.

- Never focus so intently on getting the content of your proposed Web site so perfect that you don't leave yourself an opportunity to get the site up and running so you can begin the learning curve.

- Always regard your Web site as a work in progress that is never really done, but is ever growing and changing to meet the needs and expectations of your selected market.

16

THE FUTURE OF SELECTIVE MARKETING

Now Playing at a Theater Near You

S o where is the practice of selective marketing headed, as we approach the midnight of the millennium? I moved from New York to California to find the answer to that one and after ten years of observation, I can clearly confide to you that I have seen the future and it is the emergence of "infotainment." Infotainment vehicles use information and entertainment technologies to influence specific purchase patterns. Product placement in theatrical motion pictures, infomercials, product CDs, and interactive Web sites are all practical applications of the infotainment paradigm.

SMART utilized an infotainment vehicle to influence violent gang factions for the Los Angeles City Attorney's Gang Prosecution Unit (see Chapter 5). Video distribution was the "info-"; the stage play, *Crossfire,* was the "-tainment." The result was the gang treaty between the Crips and the Bloods. For enthusiasts of Athearn Miniature Trains, we created an ongoing, on-line soap opera of the rails, with hyperlinks to product info–based Web sites (see Chapter 15). California afforded us easy access to the talents and technicians that made these early infotainment applications practical.

Our Los Angeles location also offers SMART high-level access to the entertainment industry through our client relationships with

Tri-Star, Turner, Motown, Paramount, and Disney. Our interest in the entertainment industry stems from the industry's long and successful use of market segmentation in promoting its products.

Music markets have been split into classical, jazz, pop, rock, R & B, and country and western audience segments since the early 1940s. Today, niche markets such as "alternative," "dance," and "urban contemporary" further segment the music industry.

SONY PICTURES SPOTLIGHTS WHAT MAY LIE AHEAD

Bob Levin and I worked together 20 years ago on Sears campaigns at McCann-Erickson in Chicago. Then he left to become worldwide head of marketing at the Walt Disney Company, and I went back to New York to create campaigns for Purina Cat Chow ("Chow, Chow, Chow"), Diet Coke ("Just for the Taste of It"), and Ford Motor Company ("Quality is Job 1").

Today, Levin is president of worldwide marketing at Sony Pictures and, as a motion picture executive, he is at the top of one of the foremost show business conglomerates. In December 1997, Sony Pictures and its Tri-Star and Columbia Pictures divisions were far ahead of the other studios. They had a 22 percent share of the motion picture box office for the year and their remake of *Godzilla* was being touted as the summer blockbuster of 1998. As a result of his experience, Levin brings a strong, brand-related point of view to any discussion related to the future of selective marketing. He readily concedes that "mass marketing is dead, but not the mass market." Sony reaches that mass market by appealing to each of the key segments that make up the whole. Subteens, teens, young adults, Gen-Xers, boomers, African Americans, Hispanics, Asians, and alternative lifestyles are all selected markets under Bob Levin's direct control.

Selective Marketing Goes Hollywood

When asked about the importance of selective marketing to Sony Pictures, Bob did not mince words. "Market segmentation has become increasingly important in motion pictures at an accelerated pace, due to the fragmentation of media. We in the motion picture business have had to look at ways to attract an audience to our films, understanding how media behavior is different along various markets," he confided. "Each motion picture is very different so the application of selective marketing is not that simple. One thing all major box office successes ($100 million +) have had in common was the ability to appeal to a wide variety of identifiable market segments. But in the marketing of those hit movies you may find a very specific message that attracts a young male. That message may be very distinct from a message for the same movie geared to attract the older female audience," according to Levin.

"We use market segmentation quite a bit in the development of our creative materials. Also the studio follows the same suit in its media buys utilizing sports buys for an older male audience, MTV buys for a teen audience and daytime TV buys for an older female audience. We will amass a mass market, but we will do it by appealing to specific segments of the audience with specific messages in specific media parts." This is how Levin sums up the studio's segmented marketing approach to the so-called mass market. But that is not Sony Pictures' only use of selective marketing techniques.

Lights, Camera, Segmentation!

Certain motion pictures are developed with a specific audience or market segment in mind. A movie may be slanted to an African-American audience or to teenage girls and have little or no chance of attracting a wider share of viewership. By utilizing specifically targeted media and creative messages, Sony cuts down on the high cost of wasted impressions and can make a bigger splash where it counts.

These segment-specific motion pictures are becoming of increasing interest to companies in search of promotional partners for brands that appeal to the audience such a film is geared to attract. In the case of the film, *The Mask of Zorro,* Sony Pictures received interest in copromotion from firms such as Dos Equis beer and Old El Paso salsa, trying to capitalize on the film's obvious interest potential among the Hispanic audience.

"The motion picture industry is getting a wake-up call in 1997," confides Bob Levin. He is referring to the general sense among the major studios and reflected in some statistics (probably misinterpreted) that the movie audience is getting older. The fact that boomers are getting older yet are still maintaining their youthful interest in movies (unlike the previous generation) led the studios to perceive that a larger share of viewers is older. It is the application of selective market expertise that revealed to Sony that, in fact, the largest single market segment for motion pictures comprises basically "very dynamic" 18- to 24-year-old young adults who are still single, who are better educated, and who live in larger urban markets. According to Levin, they are the people who "come out early and don't necessarily have to wait for word-of-mouth. They're more adventurous in their tastes. More interested in the social activity of just going to the movies and getting out of the house."

Movies are made for lots of different audiences, but to be a $100-million (or more) blockbuster, a movie must attract an audience of people 16 years old and and older. Levin cites that there is less risk in making a comedy for younger adults than one for older adults. In fact, he categorizes the most responsive audience (the one that sees a movie soonest) as being teenage girls, stating, "If teen girls want to see a movie they get out there the earliest, they see it again and again and they come in packs. And usually where you find teen girls you will find teen boys."

In the future, as we see it at SMART, the search for these early-adapter market segments will be driving brands in product categories other than entertainment, as companies launch new product and line extension efforts. There are lessons to be learned from the motion picture industry in product restaging and reformulation activities as well.

The movie industry taps its early adapters for information and feedback on everything from marketing materials to plot points and sometimes uses multiple finales to determine which one draws the most favorable audience response. In fact, several studios have engaged SMART to pretest motion pictures before production begins for the selected audience's feedback on storylines, casting elements, and location considerations. This makes a lot of sense, considering the tens of millions of dollars that are at stake in the production, prints, and advertising of a major motion picture.

For the larger spectrum of mass marketers investigating selective marketing practices and procedures, the movie business offers a foreshadowing of trends to come. In Hollywood, a product is created with consideration given to its targeted consumer's wants, needs, and desires. This practice will probably find more and more practical applications in other consumer markets as time goes on. We are already beginning to see increased "consumerization" of personal computers, phone services, packaged goods, automobiles, and health care products.

It is also quite likely that the use of consumer information based upon definable market segmentation will come into more prominent play in new product development programs. High school students will have a hand in developing the products they will use after they graduate from college or technical school. Parents will play a part in defining the types of products their children will come to rely upon in order to become educated. Workers will define the tools with which their employers provide them. Media will help manufacturers better understand specific audience traits and societal patterns while creating and reinforcing those same traits and patterns.

Every Movie Is a Business

Motion pictures go into business to successfully manage the exploitation of a given intellectual property for as long as possible. A $40-million investment can tank over a single weekend. An $11-million investment can yield hundreds of millions of dollars. Bob Levin tells us that a major motion picture has three days to prove itself in wide release. Once a film drops below fifth rank at the box office, it drops off the radar. That is a very short product cycle indeed.

In the future, certain product cycles, such as movie release windows, will get shorter and shorter, while usage patterns accelerate and diversify. Information will flow faster. Consumer decisions will become more informed. Word of mouth will become critical to success and endemic to failure within each selected market.

A Few Words on Word of Mouth

If a hit movie takes years to develop and produce but has a make-or-break window of no more than three days in which to prove itself, then word of mouth becomes critical to the success of every film in its respective marketplace.

Word of mouth, however, cannot be manipulated. For example, there are people in every workplace who are, as Levin says, "the local Siskel and Ebert." Such people usually tell the crowd what is good or bad and they generally have quite a local following, which makes them difficult for the studios to influence. Levin recalls overhearing a woman who, after seeing a very popular film, exclaimed to her husband, "I didn't like it very much, but I'm probably wrong because everybody else seemed to like it."

In Levin's opinion, the fact that a dissenting opinion can be influenced or changed in the face of popular support may indicate that success and popularity might have as much to do with positive word of mouth as does quality. This theory bears much consideration. If *popularity* rather than *perceived quality* influences word of mouth, then the rugged individualism of traditional values may be giving way to the herd mentality so typical of less democratic societies. If this comes to pass, then word of mouth may lose its power to influence change and instead will become a tool for maintaining order and the status quo. For those engaged in the practice of selective marketing, these subtle changes in a market segment's decision-making process warrant close observation. They will have significant bearing on our methods in the future.

THE STRANGE AMALGAM OF ART AND COMMERCE

Another reason for looking at the motion picture industry for some indicators about the future of selective marketing is Hollywood's very nature as a business model. A feature film will come together as a business for two or three years, raising tens of millions of dollars in capital based solely on the reputations and past performances of its principals, and has the potential to go on to earn (or lose) hundreds of millions of dollars for its investors. The "Hollywood Model" corporate structure of project-oriented work teams is the prototype for the much-touted virtual corporation espoused to be the economic engine of the new millennium. Participants in these new-age companies will increasingly come to look at their endeavors as an amalgam, or melding, of their particular expertise or "art" and the disciplines of running a business- or commerce-based enterprise, much as those in the major motion picture studio communities do today.

A simple dynamic drives such companies. "There has never been a bad motion picture," Bob Levin contends. "No matter how bad the worst picture you ever saw was, there is still somebody somewhere who liked it." As a result of this, Levin and his marketing staffs at Tri-Star and Columbia begin the process of turning an artistic vision into a motion picture at the same time the studio begins the determination of how much bringing that vision to life will cost. "That is the point that you must begin to deal with the realities of exactly what is the potential for the movie," Bob confides.

This does not mean making value judgments about the artistic merits of the script, but determining the economic equations attached to the proposed production. A smaller budget ($10 million or less) represents one level of marketing ambition and audience acceptance to earn its money back and declare a profit. A $75-million production budget sets up an entirely different set of parameters, marketing expenditures, and audience acceptance needs.

Into both of these equations the marketability and playability factors must be figured. Levin defines *marketability* as the inherent ideas present in the film that, prior to anyone seeing this movie, can attract an audience. This includes elements such as the concept, genre, or casting, along with the power of Sony's marketing executives to convey these benefits to the film's selected audiences. *Playability* is the level of satisfaction the filmmakers deliver to the audience that leads to the word of mouth discussed earlier.

In the future, selective marketability will lead to new product ideas conceived with an eye toward elements known to appeal to specific consumers' taste, color, usage, texture, or aromatic preferences. A page taken from the studio's selection and development process may lead to the use of specific structures in product development aimed toward certain markets by selective marketers in the next millennium. Just as studio executives know how many seconds you need between each scream to thrill teenage girls or how many explosions per film do it for urban adult males, automotive executives are starting to look at the exterior paint palettes that are most attractive to single professional women or the interior fabrics that appeal to college-educated African Americans.

Companies on the cutting edge of selective marketing already understand the importance of positioning their products as successful amalgams of art (product/service quality + design + integrity) and commerce (product/service price + durability + value). As each market segment matures, its own specific values and preferences fuse to create a group aesthetic. This group aesthetic encompasses the market segment's concepts of and preferences about what is and is not art.

The selective marketers' ability to meet and satisfy various market segments' definitions of art will determine the degree of commerce that will be successfully concluded. Let's call this *selective marketability*. Building a successful commercial entity around a future artistic or intellectual property (product) will provide the ability to generate and sustain market support. Let's call this *product/service playability*.

Art, commerce, selective marketability, and product/service playability are elements that SMART has found to be the key indicators of future success in selective marketing. Understanding the ever changing dynamics represented by these areas will be even more critical to the successful practice of selective marketing in years to come.

BEYOND BRAND AWARENESS LIES THE BRAND FRANCHISE

As the motion picture industry allows us some insight into the future of product planning as it relates to selective marketing, Hollywood also sheds light on the future of brand management. Traditionally, the brand has been the icon under which all the elements must play a supporting role. The principal precept upon which all brands are built is *brand immortality*—that is, product managers come and go but Levi's, Coca-Cola, and Jell-O are forever.

In Tinseltown, the only generally recognized studio brand is Disney. Moviegoers know what to expect from a Disney film. Worldwide, people know that the Disney "brand" stands for quality family entertainment. Through all its ups and downs, the products under the Disney brand name have been rock-solid constants in a world of fad and change.

"No other studio has determined a brand identity," states Bob Levin. "There is a growing strategy on the part of the Hollywood studios (including Disney) to develop copyrighted properties as brands," he reveals. This means that Terminator is a brand. Star Wars is a brand. Indiana Jones, Superman, and Aliens are all brands. The greatest movie brand of all, James Bond, Agent 007, is as well-known a superbrand as Nike or McDonald's. Each of these movie brands has gone on to become a franchise—a brands that reinvents itself periodically to maximize its sales opportunity.

Levin uses the case of the Sony Pictures blockbuster, *Men in Black,* to illustrate his point. In the summer of 1997, Sony launched *Men in Black,* a sci-fi comedic action-adventure film, starring Tommy Lee Jones and Will Smith. *MIB* came with an entire consumer products program, licensed properties from publishing to toys, and a broadcast life as a Saturday morning animated television series. Sony put *MIB* into video release just as the sequel entered into the planning stages. During this entire process, an MIB Web site kept fans informed about the progress of the entire program.

Research was done to determine the "brand essences" of *MIB* for the audiences that came and liked it. Then, instead of simply turning to a screenwriter or producer and saying, "Give us your idea about the next *Men in Black,*" Sony provided these screenwriters and producers with a path of consumer likes and dislikes based on their initial encounters with the MIB brand. Determining what

Men in Black meant to its selected audiences is the key to helping the creative team to build upon the property's brand strengths and avoid the MIB brand's perceived weaknesses.

"To build *Men in Black* from a hit film into a brand franchise we will have to be true to what the audiences loved about MIB, not another artist's creative vision," maintains Bob Levin. This is a major shift in thinking for the motion picture industry. It puts marketing—selective marketing—in the driver's seat for maintaining the box office success rates of Hollywood's proven performers.

SMART sees the future of brand management as likewise shifting as an ever segmenting universe of niche markets demands more franchise building than impression-generating strategy.

James Bond fans enjoy a personal relationship with their selected movie brand. They have rejected the Timothy Dalton and George Lazenby versions of the brand; they seem to have accepted the Roger Moore and Pierce Brosnan versions. The brand was, of course, defined by the performances of Sean Connery. Any casting decision not consistent with that original brand image is not accepted by the brand's market.

Corvette owners and Macintosh users enjoy a personal relationship with their selected automobile or computer platform. Those who generally like Ben & Jerry's can be counted on to hate Microsoft—Ben and Jerry push consumer buttons that Bill Gates can't reach. This is why segment-by-segment research will play an even larger role in brand management. These are all complex emotional preferences that are growing as wider segments of our nation's population gain even more access to information regarding the subjects that interest them. Here's how we see these interests developing into brand franchises in the next decade:

- Information will create value judgments.
- Value judgments will lead to opinions and preferences.
- Preferences will change over time.

- Adaptability to ever changing consumer wants and preferences will determine whether consumer/brand relationships are ongoing.

- Over time, ongoing consumer relationships supported by evolutionary selective marketing will develop into lifelong brand franchises.

AND NOW FOR THE BAD NEWS

Hollywood is not without its dark side. There is no process for damage control when one of these $40-million overnight brands begins to go south. The money has already been spent. The realities of the motion picture business today are governed by the industry's tremendous access to movie screens. To compete with network television, motion picture exhibitors had to dramatically increase the number of locations and the number of screens at those locations all across the nation.

Hence, the proliferation of multiplex theaters and the use of network and spot television commercials to promote viewer anticipation of upcoming movies. The costs for this are staggering. In fact, the marketing plans for launching most wide-release theatrical motion pictures look more like those for launching a national political campaign, according to Bob Levin. "The real war is fought in those first three days," he reiterates.

For the most part (and Levin allows for rare exceptions), if you are opening a big movie on lots of screens across the country and have already spent significant marketing dollars to build opening box-office demand and you're not in the "win" window or a good "place" position, you are virtually out of business. Being in third place is a hard spot from which to build momentum. It's very difficult to recover from an unsuccessful opening in fourth or fifth place such as the controversial *Amistad* experienced (fifth place opening week, then oblivion). Levin credits this dynamic to the public's love of supporting "winners" and the heightened awareness of box-office standings.

For those of us who look to the entertainment industry and its success at attracting young consumers in hopes of gaining a glimpse of things to come, this is most disturbing. A world of instant brands and eternally evolving product incarnations does not seem consistent with multi-million-dollar front-loaded investment spending or, for that matter, with from-the-gut market rollouts. But, unfortunately, it is. In the quest to combine art and commerce, many key decisions are left to the prerogatives of the art side, because the people there are perceived as being the ones with "vision."

Selective marketing tells us that the true vision rests with the selected consumer of the intended product or service. When a product (such as the "new" Coke) or a film (such as *Heaven's Gate*) tanks, it is usually the result of ignoring the vision of the various consumers that make up the potential market.

WHICH BRINGS US BACK TO THE CONVERGENCE OF INFORMATION AND ENTERTAINMENT

More accurately, it brings us back to the idea of information as entertainment. In the next millennium we will be educated and entertained simultaneously. This process will be rapid, ongoing, multileveled, and, for the most part, commerce-oriented. The lessons learned from today's make-or-break world of movie production may well determine tomorrow's category leaders in baby formula and bathroom cleaners.

Even as motion picture studio marketing and production executives hire SMART to test the marketability and playability elements of their recently developed intellectual property brands for audience reactions among various selective market segments, advertisers are enlisting us to develop intellectual property vehicles that enhance and dimensionalize their product brands. Indications are that these infotainment arenas are the frontiers at which America will reinvent itself and its products in the coming age.

Therefore, we offer the following advice in closing. To be in step with the tides of change, don't search far and wide, look close and dig deep. To win big, think small. And to conquer the mass market, don't start by lumping everybody together based upon vague similarities. Start by dividing groups of consumers into segments based upon specific, usable differences. Put simply, the future of marketing is to divide the mass market into segments and to conquer, one by one, those most inclined to be your customers. Happy hunting.

Index